DEMOCRACY AND CONSTITUTIONS

Putting Citizens First

As things stand, a commitment to weak democracy and strong constitutionalism ensures that a range of elite groups, actors, and institutions – political, economic, intellectual, and legal – hold considerable sway over constitutional matters, leaving less room for the participation of ordinary people. With the continued primacy of liberal constitutionalism, constitutional law has come to represent and facilitate the centrality of judicial power and authority. In *Democracy and Constitutions*, Allan C. Hutchinson warns against this deference to a legal elite on questions of constitutional meaning. For Hutchinson, an over-reliance on constitutional law, and a lack of attention to democratic politics, keeps people from influencing the moral and political character of society; it saps civic energies and relegates ordinary people to the sidelines.

Engaging and provocative, *Democracy and Constitutions* charts a course away from the elitism of the present and toward a more democratic future, one that re-balances society's commitment to both democracy and constitutions. Advocating for a strong democracy and weak constitutionalism, this book places ordinary people at the institutional heart of government and politics, arguing that such a re-calibration is better for democracy and for society.

ALLAN C. HUTCHINSON is a distinguished research professor at the Osgoode Hall Law School, York University.

⌕ UTP insights

UTP Insights is an innovative collection of brief books offering accessible introductions to the ideas that shape our world. Each volume in the series focuses on a contemporary issue, offering a fresh perspective anchored in scholarship. Spanning a broad range of disciplines in the social sciences and humanities, the books in the UTP Insights series contribute to public discourse and debate and provide a valuable resource for instructors and students.

For a list of books published in the series, please see page 207.

DEMOCRACY AND CONSTITUTIONS

Putting Citizens First

Allan C. Hutchinson

UNIVERSITY OF TORONTO PRESS
Toronto Buffalo London

ISBN 978-1-4875-0792-3 (cloth)   ISBN 978-1-4875-3723-4 (EPUB)
ISBN 978-1-4875-0793-0 (paper)   ISBN 978-1-4875-3722-7 (PDF)

Library and Archives Canada Cataloguing in Publication

Title: Democracy and constitutions : putting citizens first /
Allan C. Hutchinson.

Names: Hutchinson, Allan C., 1951– author.

Series: UTP insights.

Description: Series statement: UTP insights | Includes bibliographical
references and index.

Identifiers: Canadiana (print) 20210157658 | Canadiana (ebook)
20210157798 | ISBN 9781487507930 (paper) | ISBN 9781487507923 (cloth) |
ISBN 9781487537227 (PDF) | ISBN 9781487537234 (EPUB)

Subjects: LCSH: Constitutional law. | LCSH: Democracy.

Classification: LCC K3165.H88   2021 | DDC 342.02–dc23

The Book of Laughter and Forgetting by Milan Kundera. Copyright © Milan
Kundera, 1978, used by permission of The Wylie Agency (UK) Limited.

University of Toronto Press acknowledges the financial assistance to its
publishing program of the Canada Council for the Arts and the Ontario
Arts Council, an agency of the Government of Ontario.

Canada Council   Conseil des Arts
for the Arts   du Canada

ONTARIO ARTS COUNCIL
CONSEIL DES ARTS DE L'ONTARIO

an Ontario government agency
un organisme du gouvernement de l'Ontario

A2J⁵

"The struggle of man against power is the struggle of memory against forgetting."

– Milan Kundera

Contents

Preface

I wrote this book during the tempestuous times of a Donald Trump presidency and its "Make America Great Again" mantra. On such a challenging occasion, the importance of democracy and constitutions seemed even more important than ever. The tendency of many jurists and political commentators was to turn to the Constitution and the courts in order to curb the disorienting forces of Trump's brand of democratic populism (which itself was little more than a front for a divisive and authoritarian sectarianism). Some of the deep and lingering suspicions about the reach and legitimacy of democratic governance surfaced with a vengeance: it was contended that the presence of checks and balances of constitutional law was needed now more than ever before. A similar situation was also taking place in Canada with the rise of Doug Ford's premiership in Ontario.

In this book, I want to take a very different tack. While I am as critical as anyone about this disastrous turn in politics and its debasement of democratic ideals and practices, I insist that the response ought not to be a resort to courts and a dilution of democratic commitments. Indeed, I maintain that it is not less democracy that we need, but more democracy. While the constitution has a role to play in a strong democracy, the increase in resorting to it and relying upon its judicial enforcers is not the road to follow. Indeed, the courts have not always been willing to stand up for democracy or even the Constitution in checking government excess and even a turn towards authoritarianism. Instead, there is an urgent need for a fresh and robust reinvigoration of democratic processes and institutions. It is not democracy that is the problem. Despite efforts by Trump and his cronies to undermine the democratic process and to persist with a baseless assault on its outcome, democracy did manage to prevail, if barely.

Nor is it that constitutional law is the answer. There should be a thorough rethinking of the relationship between democracy and constitutions. In short, I contend that, in place of the present acceptance of strong constitutionalism and weak democracy, a concerted effort must be made to strengthen the force of democracy in society and weaken the grip of a constitutionalist approach to political governance. A democratic impulse and practice is always preferable to elitist ones, no matter how progressive or well-intentioned. Accordingly, this book pushes for an unrelenting commitment to the goal of a truly democratic system of government in both form and substance; it avoids the false allure of constitutional government.

My own commitment to democracy has occasionally succumbed to the temptations and blandishments of an elitist constitutionalism. As a law professor, I deal with and sometimes get lost in the details of constitutional politics and the ins-and-outs of Supreme Court jurisprudence. However, there have always been friends and colleagues who have pulled me up short and reminded me of the elitist error of my ways. I am truly grateful to them and their persistence. At the top of that list are Andrew Petter and Joel Colon-Rios. In their different styles, Andrew and Joel have been both wonderful co-authors and loyal critics. I am most grateful to their friendship, forbearance, and insight. Also, my old friends Rob Thorpe and Paul Brown have recently reminded me of my roots in a Manchester milieu of the 1960s and 1970s when a belief in the idea of "a better life for all" seemed both inspiring and almost taken-for-granted in our coming of age – "ta very much, lads."

As always, I have also benefited from the support and generosity of family, friends, and colleagues. I will refrain from listing them in order to protect them from any charges of complicity in my scholarly exploits. That said, I simply record my genuine thanks for all they do in making my work possible and enjoyable. I am grateful to the anonymous readers at the University of Toronto Press; their comments and provocations made this a better book. Also, I am very appreciative to the members of my 2020 seminar "Democracy and Constitutions" for their energetic challenges and proposals to improve this project. Finally, I have relied on students and research assistants in making less errors than I might otherwise have done. Elias Rabinovitch, Nicole Daniels, Neil MacIsaac, Tomislav Milos, and Molly Martin merit a deserved shout-out.

January 2021

DEMOCRACY AND CONSTITUTIONS

Putting Citizens First

chapter one

Democracy and Constitutions: Laughing and Forgetting

Since its limited introduction in Greece in the sixth century BC, democracy as a preferred mode of politics and governance has come a long way. It extends to more citizens (not only privileged males) and includes more aspects of governance. Yet, for all its increase in reach and depth in the intervening millennia, democracy still remains today an attenuated idea and incomplete practice. Even its flag-bearers are often long on supportive rhetoric, but short on decisive action; they are too open to restricting democracy's appeal and application in favour of some distinct conception of political morality. In particular, there has been a continuing effort to put democracy in the service of liberalism: liberal democracy is viewed as democracy *tout court*. In the process, democracy has been both sidelined and side-stepped; citizens play little role in government even though they are often reminded of their privileged status in a democratic society.

This tendency is especially marked in the conflicted and central relation between democracy and constitutions. In Canada and the United States, the historical arc of law and politics has been significantly determined by the extent to which democracy has been both advanced and restrained by the demands of liberal constitutionalism. The general outcome of this institutional tension has been that there is a definite preference for a strong constitutionalism over weak democracy. Indeed, the liberal defenders of such an alignment maintain that this is not a betrayal or even cramping of the democratic ideal, but is actually the best way to fulfil the

broader ambitions of a serious commitment to democratic governance. Such scholarly commentators and political actors believe
that, if democracy is to work as a practical and prominent template
for modern government, it must be disciplined and structured in
the name of other important and more defensible political values.

In this book, I want to take a different and opposing position.
I insist that there needs to be an institutional turnabout – there
should be strong democracy and weak constitutionalism. As things
presently stand, a commitment to weak democracy and strong constitutionalism ensures that a range of elite groups and institutions –
political, economic, intellectual, legal, and more – hold great sway
over the polity and its commitment to the increased participation
of ordinary people in governmental matters. In particular, the most
disturbing effect of the continuing primacy of liberal constitutionalism has been that constitutional law has come to represent and
facilitate "the arrogation of unlimited power by the judges."[1] This
does not mean that all judicial decisions (and the musings of their
juristic aides) are consistently bad in substance and effect; some
constitutional jurisprudence will and should garner widespread
support and popular acceptance.

However, this entrenched deference to a legal elite on questions of constitutional meaning makes justice and fairness, at best,
into an act of *noblesse oblige*. The reliance on constitutional law (as
opposed to democratic politics) robs people of their entitlement
to be the main source of society's moral and political guidance; it
saps civic energies and relegates ordinary people to also-rans. This
state of affairs is to be lamented, especially when it is defended
in the name of democracy itself. Accordingly, there is an urgent
need to rebalance society's commitment to democracy and constitutions. In short, it would be much better if there was an informing
dynamic of strong democracy and weak constitutionalism. This
will serve to place ordinary people more at the institutional heart
of government and politics: it will ensure that governance is not
simply a matter *for* and *of* the people, but will also be *by* the people.
In contrast to present-day governmental arrangements and activities, it is the constitution that must be understood and placed in the
service of democracy, not vice versa.

Of Democracies and Constitutions

Constitutionalism preceded democracy. The main elements of most societies' constitutional orders were firmly in place before all persons were treated as citizens and before the franchise was extended to all those citizens. For instance, in the United States and Canada, although the fundamental constitutional compact was in place by 1791 and in 1867, respectively, the final extension of the franchise did not take place until much later in the 1960s. Yet, even today, the percentage of the voting-age population who actually vote in federal elections remains alarmingly low. It reached a modest peak of over 60 per cent in the 1950s and 1960s, dropped to lows of less than 60 per cent, and is now back in the low 60 per cent range: these figures are much lower for local, state, and provincial elections. However, despite the historical priority of constitutionalism and continuing low electoral participation, the growth of democracy as both an idea and practice has raised pressing concerns for political and legal theorists. In particular, while the structures and details of constitutional orders have developed and changed over time, the challenge of increased popular participation has obliged a re-examination of the appropriate and legitimate relationship between constitutionalism and democracy. This relationship is clearly contested and complicated. It raises a number of deep issues and concerns: Are democracy and constitutionalism necessarily complementary or contradictory? Can there be a mode of "constitutional democracy" that is both coherent and reliable in effecting social justice? Can democracy be left to its own devices without a disciplinary constitutional structure and process?

The central notion of constitutionalism is that, although government is established to serve popular interests, government must be constrained in its powers if it is to retain authority in exercising those powers. As such, constitutions not only organize and distribute power, they place limits upon its exercise. In its predominantly liberal incarnation, there is a strong belief that there must be procedural and substantive limits placed on what policies the citizens can require or expect their political institutions to pursue. Indeed, these constraints on contingent democratic demands can be seen as the foundational and enabling conditions for an enduring and virtuous democratic polity. In this vision, democracy is not the main process by which political justice is constituted or achieved, but is merely instrumental to the preservation and expression of that goal. There is, of course, much debate among constitutionalists about the nature and extent of these limitations. Some of the most common arrangements relied upon to achieve such a balance of power and accountability include the familiar notions of separation of powers, adherence to the Rule of Law, constitutional supremacy, and, of course, the protection of fundamental rights through judicial review. As John Rawls, the leading modern liberal constitutionalist argued, in a constitutional regime with judicial review, public reason is the reason of its supreme court.[2]

These basic features of modern constitutionalism have much to recommend them and have become accepted as the *sine qua non* of good governance. However, this is not the whole story. Constitutionalism is also characterized by an obsession with permanence, a resistance to constitutional change, and a deep suspicion of popular assemblies and direct participation. Underlying many constitutionalist theories is the idea that, once the constitution contains the right abstract principles and the correct balance of institutional safeguards, it is a good and finished constitution. There is room for fine-tuning in the details of its operation and implementation as circumstances change, but there is no need or warrant for further changes of a substantial or structural kind. Indeed, the claim is that to alter the constitutional arrangements in significant ways is to look for political trouble, to play with the stability of the governance system, and to risk the precious ideal of the Rule of Law. Moreover, the rise of democracy and the spread of popular entitlement has heightened those fears.

Of course, what it means to promote "democracy" and to incorporate its demands into a society's scheme of government is highly contested. At the heart of that dispute is the role of "popular participation." The dominant view in both theory and practice has been that a commitment to democracy does not have to entail a decisive or central role for popular participation; it is a necessary feature of any democratic society, but it is not its final or superior mode of governmental authority. Indeed, popular participation has been relegated to a distinctly second-best position in modern systems of so-called democratic governance. In particular, it is objected that the proposed limits on popular power are not and cannot be self-executing and must be determined by some institutional device, usually some form of judicial review. The traditional fear is that, if popular participation is left unregulated and uninhibited, it will result in acts and policies that are antithetical to social justice and even democratic ideals more broadly conceived. For instance, the majoritarian trampling of minority rights is the most commonly cited and feared consequence of unchecked democracy.

These concerns about popular participation are not trivial or entirely unproven. However, they are by no means inevitable or unavoidable; they are insufficient on their own to undermine the case for a robust commitment to a strong form of democracy that places popular participation at its dynamic heart. In contrast to weak democrats, the strong democrat insists that there is no philosophical authority or analytical method for "illuminating truths" that is somehow a separate process from a democratic society's own efforts to act justly and fairly and that can itself underwrite those efforts. Accordingly, because there is no neutral or privileged way to trump popular participation as a process through which to debate and formulate what policies to pursue, the justification for the need to place traditional restraints on popular authority are unconvincing. Moreover, popular participation is not (or need not be) as unprincipled, arbitrary, or self-serving as many constitutionalists suggest. At its more uncompromising, therefore, the democratic critique of constitutionalism is that it operates, as Tocqueville foresaw, more as a cover for elite control and facilitates a tyranny of the few over the many. In a strong democracy, political legitimacy is more appropriately secured by obtaining direct consent from active citizens; there is no need for subsequent validation through abstract reasoning from philosophical mentors or detached consideration by judicial proconsuls. In short, strong democracy and constitutionalism (or "weak democracy") have very different attitudes and approaches to the wisdom and reliability of popular politics.

In line with this insight, this book insists that the primary tension in legal and political theory should not be between constitutionalism and democracy *per se*, but between different accounts of constitutionalism in terms of their willingness to place more or less confidence in democratic politics in the pursuit of a just system of governance. In short, in a constitutional democracy and in contested matters of political morality, the central question is whether the prosaic or primary location of authority and legitimacy is to be found in an entrenched constitutional order or in the regular participation of citizens. Under the tutelage of the analytical tradition, legal theorists have tended to view this question as primarily philosophical in scope and substance. However, I am recommending that the largely neglected historical, political, and strategic aspects of this inquiry demand much greater attention. Indeed, despite the frequently trumpeted value and importance of democracy in modern politics, its institutional imperatives and normative significance have been treated as decidedly inferior in the constitutional scheme of things: the chronological precedence of constitutionalism has been endowed with continuing and unwarranted conceptual priority by modern commentators and officials.

It can be fairly reported that modern legal and political theory displays a discernible uneasiness towards the thrust and influence of a democratic commitment that is both *for* the people and *by* the people. Democrats stand for most of what constitutionalists fear or dislike. Unlike constitutionalists, they do not contend that the purpose of constitutional democracy is to protect democracy from itself. Indeed, many constitutionalists only manage to pass themselves off as democrats because they shave the idea of democracy so thin that they transform constitutionalism into the democratic *telos*. In contrast, strong democrats maintain that "rule by the people" recommends at least two general and indispensable commitments on the constitutional front – (1) an institutional *openness* in which even the most fundamental principles are amenable to popular discussion and are always susceptible to being reformulated or replaced; and (2) an empowerment of people so that they come together in political equality and settle on the laws that will regulate the institutions and practices under which they live. In order for these rules to be the people's own, it must be today's people who rule, not past generations: the constitutionalist idea of pre-commitment cannot be brought to any final or fixed reconciliation with democracy. If people are to rule themselves and not be ruled by others, no matter how benign or beneficial their objectives and values, it is imperative that strong constitutionalists step aside and make way for strong democrats.

Failing to Remember

As one of the most contested and capacious concepts in the political lexicon, "democracy" can and has been used to promote all manner of different and often competing ideas and practices. This is both good and bad. While it is now the case that being a democrat is considered to be a positive and almost unavoidable identity in political struggle, it means that it hides as much as it illuminates. In a world of diverse opinions and values, it is treated as both a process and a substantive measure of political engagement. So much is justified in the name of democracy: it offers itself as a grand motivating ambition and the source of the limits and constraints on that vision. As Agnes Repplier famously phrased it, "democracy forever teases us with the contrast between its ideals and its realities, between its heroic possibilities and its sorry achievements."[3] The history of democracy (and its relation to constitutionalism) is in so many ways a history of modern North American society. Accordingly, in this book, I intend to examine both democracy's ideal and real possibilities as well as its heroic and sorry achievements. This is a considerable undertaking, but one that must be done. To do so, I will call in aid the stimulating and unsettling ideas of the Czech writer, Milan Kundera.

Milan Kundera is no easy read. His sophisticated writings demand serious engagement by their readers. In so demanding, he asks his readers to take themselves out of their comfort zone and put themselves at risk. His work is an unapologetic act of provocation and bravura – intellectual, political, psychological, sexual, and personal. As with other great stylists, he sashays confidently along the perilous line between the obscure and the profound, the ridiculous and the sublime, and the reassuring and disturbing. Yet Kundera is as distinct in his writings as he is universal. He integrates autobiography with literary imagination to assemble a cast of characters and set of narratives that are as harrowing as they are emancipatory. He uses his idiosyncratic creations to illuminate and indict the foibles of humankind in a contemporary world that works in complex and irreducible ways both to liberate and dominate its fragile citizens. It is fair to say that Kundera's *oeuvre* is a signal, if contested, achievement insofar as it meets as well as strives to transform the standards of literary performance and possibility.

In one of his most celebrated efforts, *The Book of Laughter and Forgetting*, Kundera draws on his own Czech experience of Russian oppression in the 1960s and 1970s. With the blessings and blights of being an exile from his Czech homeland, he manages to mine insights and intuitions about the human condition more generally. The text is a mediation on and an incitement to confront the inescapable pain as well as the redemptive power of memory and laughter. In particular, in a loosely, yet deeply connected series of vignettes, he traverses both the personal and political terrain on which his characters struggle to make sense of things. He is both brutal and empathetic in his exploration: he spares neither his protagonists nor himself in his efforts to address and discern the often incomprehensible limits and openings of modern living. In particular, with irony and realism, Kundera fixates on how memory – national, institutional, collective, and individual – works to maintain and mangle people's efforts to make sense of themselves and others in critical moments of crisis, upheaval, and reconstruction. Although he talks of both laughter and forgetting, there is little that is comical or escapist in his disconcerting reflections and tropic designs.

Memory – both its vulnerabilities and its vanities – is at the heart of Kundera's book. He understands how its preservation and selectivity is essential to society and individuals as they make and remake their lives. However, for him, tyranny begins and is built upon the erasure and replacement of collective memory. The *modus operandi* of the tyrannical regime is "to efface thousands of lives from memory and leave nothing but an unstained age of unstained idyll": it is the effort to "want to be masters of the future only for the power to change the past" so that "the future [cannot] be weighed down by memory." In Kundera's own case, when the Russians invaded the Czech Republic in 1968, it began by silencing the nation's historians so as to ensure that resistance and its heroic agents were "erased from the country's memory, like mistakes in the school child's homework." Instead, a "desert of organized forgetting" with only the "melancholy flowers of forgetting" was cultivated by the oppressors. As he puts it:

> You begin to liquidate a people ... by taking away its memory. You destroy its books, its culture, its history. And then others write other books for it, give another culture to it, invent another history for it. Then the people slowly begins to forget what it is and what it was. The world at large forgets it still faster.[4]

On an individual level, Kundera explores the pernicious effects and tricks of memory on people's identity in their efforts to reclaim and reconstitute themselves. In chronicling Tamina's life, a thirty-three-year-old café waitress in Prague, he plays out this political dynamic on a more personal level and captures the disorienting impact of memory and forgetting:

> She tried initially to recover memories that could serve as reference points in time's flow and become the underlying framework of a reconstructed past ... because if the tottering structure of her memories collapses like a clumsily pitched tent, all that [we] will be left with is the present, that invisible point, that nothingness moving slowly toward death.[5]

Although Kundera's canvas is much darker and more disturbing than my own, I want to examine how the effects of memory and forgetting play out in the world of democracy and constitutions, especially in North America. The accepted history of constitutionalism and democracy in the United States and Canada is a function of erasure and amnesia. It would be taking things too far and be too paranoid for me to think that there was a "desert of organized forgetting." The history of constitutions and democracy is less organized, less hopeless, and less comprehensive than that. Yet memory and forgetting play a formative role in contemporary understandings about both our constitutional and democratic past and our constitutional and democratic present and future. People have lost (and, to varying degrees, been obliged to lose) the authentic memories of how our constitutions arose, how they have played out over 200 years or more, and the promise and possibilities of their future reconstruction.

While the received historical thread is about constitutional occasions of democratic birth and their better and purifying development, the realities are much less reassuring; they are the stuff of collective forgetting. It is only through understanding the efforts and effects of this institutional forgetting and the continuing erasure of memory that present commitments and future movements around democracy and constitutions can be appreciated and changed. Accordingly, in this book, I want to revisit the constitutional past and explore its present in order to develop a better and more democratic future. In this sense, my project is to reclaim historical memory and understand the role that forgetting has played in sustaining the touted glory of present constitutional arrangements. For the defenders of a constitutionalist faith, the fate of democracy is inextricably tied to the preservation of the existing constitutional structure and mindset. In contrast to that, my own ambition is to remember the constitutional past in order to reorient the present so as to work towards the future of a more democratic society.

No Laughing Matter?

In working towards this reclamation of memory and the abandonment of forgetting, I want to rely upon a devilish device that Kundera identifies and unearths in his motivating impulse towards political emancipation and personal enlightenment – *laughter*. For him, "real and total" laughter is not contrived or forced, it is "serious laughter, laughter beyond joking" that goes to the core of our being and is "without memory" – "to laugh is to live profoundly." This may seem a trivializing and perhaps laughable way to go about such a serious project as overcoming collective forgetting, as acknowledging past injustices, and as imagining a more democratic future. But this perception would be mistaken. When understood as Kundera suggests, an unsuppressed laughter can be not only the best medicine for disenfranchised societies but also the most suitable posture to take in setting about and completing the most serious and urgent task of political reconstruction for those societies.

Kundera thinks about laughter in a nuanced and ennobling way. He introduces the competing laughters of devils and angels. For him, these traditional antagonists are not as simple or as stark in their rivalry and adversarialness as many have thought or presumed. In his novelistic commentary, he presents and portrays these risible rivals more as countervailing influences than polar opposites:

> To see the devil as a partisan of Evil and angel as a warrior on the side of Good is to accept the demagogy of the angels. Things are, of course, more complicated than that. Angels are partisans not of Good but of divine creation. The devil, on the other hand, is the one who refuses to grant any rational meaning to that divinely created world.
>
> Dominion over the world, as we know it, is divided between Angels and Devils. The good of the world, however, implies not that the Angels have the advantage over the devils (as I believed when I was a child) but that the powers of the two sides are nearly in equilibrium. If there were too much incontestable meaning in the world (the angels' power), man would succumb under its weight. If the world were to lose all its meaning (the devils' reign), we could not live either.[6]

Kundera goes on to recommend that it is in their laughter (and their attitude towards it) that the character and worth of angels and devils can be most clearly grasped. In a typical Kunderian twist of irony, he insists that "throughout the world the angels had occupied all positions of authority, all the general staffs, had taken over the left and the right." This is because the angels had no capacity to engage in real laughter – "an ecstatic laughter ... without memory and without desire." The angels were consigned to offer only a "disastrous" and "laughable laughter" that worked to trick us into mistaking their complicity for virtue and rightness:

> Things deprived suddenly of their supposed meaning, of the place assigned to them in the so-called order of things, make us laugh. In origin, laughter is thus the devil's domain. It has something malicious about it (things suddenly turning out to be different from what they pretended to be), but to some extent also a beneficent relief (things are less weighty than they appeared to be, letting us live more freely, no longer oppressing us with their austere seriousness).
>
> The first time an angel heard the devil's laughter, he was dumbfounded ... The angel clearly understood that such laughter was directed against God and against the dignity of his works. He knew that he must react swiftly somehow. Unable to come up with anything of his own, he aped his adversary. Opening his mouth, he emitted broken, spasmodic sounds in the higher reaches of his vocal range ... but giving them opposite meaning: whereas the devil's laughter denoted the absurdity of things, the angel on the contrary meant to rejoice over how well ordered, wisely conceived, good, and meaningful everything here below was.
>
> Thus the angel and the devil faced each other and, mouths wide open, emitted nearly the same sounds, but each one's noise expressed the absolute opposite of the other's. And seeing the angle laugh, the devil laughed all the more, all the harder, and all the more blatantly, because the laughing angel was infinitely comical.[7]

In Kundera's register of laughter, I want to side more with the devils than the angels. As he warns, such devilish laughter is not in itself a panacea for democracy's ills. But, by leaning more towards the devilish side, I hope to draw upon its more beneficent qualities than its presumed malicious intent. My project is to work as an antidote to the hollow angelic laughter of the constitutionalists and to unsettle their dubious designs on democracy. In so doing, I strive to overcome "the deserted space of a world where the fearsome laughter of the angels rings out" and where critics often are fated to experience the "drowning out [of their] words with its jangle." Instead, I want to give voice to a form of remembering and laughter that encourages people not to "try to replace one type of power with another, [but] ... repudiate the very principle of power and repudiate it everywhere." This democratic exertion against the power of elites and others goes to the very core of what it means to be part of "the struggle of memory against forgetting."[8] This is a radical undertaking that brings into full play the crucial and enduring relation between democracy and constitutionalism as a debilitating historical enterprise and as a transformative political practice.

This book, therefore, covers a large sweep and depth of material. In doing so, it is short on overwhelming details, but longer on theme and pertinence. I begin by offering a full account of constitutionalism that is intended to be true to its own ambitions and achievements as I can. This is followed by a critical unpacking of that account that emphasizes the extent of the collective and deliberate erasure and forgetting – a historical peek at the founding moments of both the American and Canadian constitutions; an inquiry into the transcendental claims of constitutional values; and the formal and informal modes of constitutional change. This is followed by a fuller and more demanding examination, by way of two chapters, on what democracy is and can be. Then, I look at legal and scholarly efforts to make constitutions more democratic. Finally, I offer three chapters on a more practical and constructive plan for instituting a form of constitutionalism that advances rather than inhibits the full flourishing of a democratic politics. Throughout the thesis advanced in this book, the animating idea is to take democracy seriously by taking constitutionalism less seriously – a weaker constitutionalism in the service of a stronger democracy.

Conclusion

In July 1987, the American Congress held the Iran-Contra Hearings. A controversial Lieutenant-Colonel Oliver North gave testimony to the effect that he believed that blame for the ill-fated involvement of American troops in the Nicaraguan civil war was attributable to Congress's vacillation and poor policymaking. However, in a powerful and wide-ranging retort, New Hampshire's republican senator, Warren B. Rudman, stated:

> I guess the last thing I want to say to you, Colonel, is that the American people have the constitutional right to be wrong. And what Ronald Reagan thinks or what Oliver North thinks or what I think or what anybody else thinks makes not a whit if the American people say "enough." And that's why this Congress has been fickle and has vacillated. That is correct. But not because the people here necessarily believe differently than you do, but there comes a point that the views of the American people have to be heard.[9]

This retort captures much about the reformulated and dynamic idea of constitutionalism and democracy that I put forward in this book. I am not suggesting that my representation of democracy is the *real* meaning of democracy in the American or Canadian scheme of constitutionalism (or any other polity). Nor am I recommending that it is the *only* meaning to be given to constitutionalism in a democratic scheme of governance. Instead, I am proposing one way of thinking about constitutionalism that is more conducive to a vision and practice of strong democracy in the early twenty-first century North American polities of Canada and the United States – it is the voice and views of ordinary people that "have to be heard" and should carry the constitutionalist day. In the name of social and political justice, this book adopts a devilish and laughter-filled democratic approach in the task of confronting the angelic pretentions of traditional constitutionalist thinking and its concerted effort to erase memory.

chapter two

A Constitutionalist State of Mind: A Deeper Dive

All states have some form of constitution: it is what makes them into a state. All that is meant by this is that there is some scheme, formally adopted or simply informally followed, that delineates and distributes political power within a society. Some countries have elaborate and entrenched arrangements that not only do this but also map the contours of the relationship between the state and its citizens. Whether these understandings are respected or reflect the actual exercise of power on any given occasion is a matter of sociological inquiry and interest. Even the existence of written and celebrated constitutions offers evidence of aspiration or obfuscation, but little more: it does not by itself describe the conditions on the ground or the circumstances in which people live. The connection between the "law on the books" and the "law in action" is especially important as well as troublesome in regard to the effect and enforcement of constitutions. As Shakespeare's Hamlet might have put it, constitutions are often more honoured in their breach than in their observance.[1]

However, there is a particular mode of thinking about constitutions that has a more prescriptive and judgmental slant to it. This is "constitutionalism." It is an idea that has a celebrated pedigree in both political theory and historical practice. At its most basic and straightforward, it recommends that there should be a series of formal arrangements in place that not only bestow authority on particular state agencies and actors to do a range of activities, but also place enforceable constraints on the legitimate exercise of those powers. While this often involves a charter of rights and freedoms, it is not an obligatory feature of the constitutionalist mandate. That said, without adherence to this ideal, it is contended that there would be anarchy or despotism. In this chapter, I intend to canvass the core elements of that normative commitment. Although my focus will be on constitutionalism generally, I will be emphasizing and elaborating on the relation between the dominant mode of constitutionalist thinking and the limited role that it accords to "democracy" in charting the legitimacy of political action and authority.

A Constitutionalist State of Mind

With the imminent fall of the medieval order and the growing resistance to tyrannical and monarchical forms of government, the appeal of a more popular government began to take hold. While the notion of universal suffrage and widespread participation was not yet viable or anticipated, the existence of absolute and unlimited power for rulers and governments was anathema to this modernist tendency. Instead, the creation and implementation of foundational schemes that both allocated power and limited the manner and substance of its exercise became a rallying cry. Government was to be constituted and channelled within a framework that had as its primary and essential goal the imposition and maintenance of borders around the legitimate assumption and exercise of governmental power and authority. Although the strength of these constraints ebbed and flowed, the historical debate was less about whether limitations should exist but more about what character they should take: "in all its successive phases, constitutionalism has one essential quality: it is a legal limitation on government."[2] Of course, not only the substance and style of constitutionalism's limitations on government changed and shifted over the years, but the nature of government has also changed and shifted over the years.

Accordingly, this meant that a legitimate government became a constitutionally enabled government. As important, the existence and enforcement of a functioning and effective constitution also came to be understood as the *sine qua non* of good and just governance. This shift was based on the notion that, while strong and enforced constitutions could not in themselves guarantee a consistently just set of outcomes, they did offer a reasonably good chance that arbitrary governance would be controlled and that things would be better rather than worse for the state's general populace. Most importantly, the constitution was intended to be a mechanism that contained day-to-day politics by placing certain matters beyond its reach and revision: this was the case regardless of the kind of government, whether monarchical or democratic. Although constitutions have relied upon different devices to achieve this end, familiar components included separation of powers, division of powers (federalism), adherence to the Rule of Law, the judicial review of executive and legislative action, and the like.

Understood in this way, constitutionalism has been a driving rationale for the proliferation of written and formal constitutions throughout the world in the twentieth century. For instance, after the First World War, about twenty-two European countries adopted new constitutions that embodied this constitutionalist commitment. In the last two decades of the twentieth century, more than seventy countries introduced or revised their constitutions. These states were broadly spread across the globe and included Africa, Asia, and Latin America as well as former communist nations in Eastern Europe.[3] Of course, it did not necessarily follow that the underlying mandates and supposed *raison d'être* of these constitutional schemes and provisions were upheld or respected. But it represented a symbolic and sometimes significant move away from a governmental regime of often arbitrary and/or tyrannical governance. That said, even as autocratic modes of governance were abandoned in favour of more democratic alternatives, the political allure of constitutionalism persisted. It was democracy that had to accommodate itself to constitutionalism, not the other way round.

Although by no means universal in scope or acceptance, this constitutionalist momentum has been dominated by a liberal sensibility in North America. At the heart of this movement has been the drive to incorporate a series of individual rights and entitlements that are extended to citizens in their dealings with government. This is claimed to be a natural corollary of the idea of constitutions as a hedge against government tyranny or overreach. By placing people's individual freedoms outside the realm of official curtailment or interference, a state can pledge to its citizens an enduring respect for a just and responsive mode of political and social life. In line with this way of thinking, the United States has been held up as "a beacon on a hill." With a basic and enduring constitutional order that goes back almost 230 years, it projects itself as a governance model for other aspiring and evolving nations to emulate. Constitutionalism is parcelled and promoted as an ideal system that can and should be treated as the underwriter for a fair and just system, no matter the political or ideological thrust of any particular society.

As such, the key features of a modern constitutionalist approach to political governance have come to include the following central principles:

- A constitution is not to be considered to be simply one more legal, if elaborate and broad-ranging, scheme that has the same status as other laws: a constitution is a *higher* and entrenched law that takes precedence over other laws and has greater force and effect;
- Being a more fundamental law, it should only be amenable to change by a demanding and rigorous process of amendment; it will not be able to fulfil its primary purpose if it is capable of being easily and repeatedly changed as the government changes;
- As a higher law, it is understood as a neutral framework that allows day-to-day politics to be conducted along partisan and even ideological lines: a constitution is above the political fray and should itself have no particular political slant or ideological orientation;
- A constitution is concerned with the exercise and effects of public power; it does not assert authority over private power and cannot be invoked by persons in those non-public arenas. It leaves that task to the political and legitimate discretion of those in government;
- A constitution, particularly if it has a bill of rights, needs to be interpreted and applied by an independent and impartial body;

this task has generally fallen to courts and judges either by design or default; and

- Courts are expected to act in a non-ideological way in interpreting and enforcing constitutional provisions on behalf of citizens; judges are not to impose their own political agendas on a constitution's development and future direction.

Taken together, these principles are thought to be sufficient to underwrite the legitimacy of government and to offer an enduring normative basis against which to measure the legitimacy and fairness of governance. They are posited to stand as a bulwark against the interests of the general populace and against individual citizens being held hostage to oppressive or dictatorial forms of government action. Accordingly, for its champions, a constitutionalist-inspired constitution offers constraints on contingent political action and provides standards for its evaluation that together comprise the best foundational terms and conditions for the establishment and maintenance of an enduring and virtuous polity and thriving society.

What about Democracy?

For all its strengths and appeal, a glaring omission of this constitutionalist approach in both judicial opinions and scholarly texts is its treatment and attitude towards democracy. With the decline of autocratic rule and the rise of more popular governments, democracy has been a powerful idea and practice in the twentieth century. Most constitutions contain provisions that guarantee the rights of all citizens to participate in elections as both voters and representatives; this is not to be scoffed at or underrated. Nevertheless, most constitutions do little to advance a more ample vision of democratic ideals in any direct or significant way. Indeed, it seems to be a general thrust of a constitutionalist approach that democracy is something to be guarded against rather than enhanced.

Within such a constitutionalist scheme, the claims of democracy as a regulative ideal seem to be lost. It would seem that not only did constitutionalism predate democracy as a historical fact, but that it continues to be granted prior and greater significance in the constitutionalists' lexicon – constitutionalism is, at best, served by democracy rather than being a service to democracy; democracy is secondary and subservient to constitutionalism. Indeed, one prominent liberal constitutionalist goes so far as to conclude that "a perfectly just constitutional regime would be legitimate even in the absence of consent."[4] This strikes a very familiar chord in the constitutionalist debate. It is not that such theorists are averse or antagonistic to democracy in itself. Indeed, they take the audacious view that an attachment to constitutionalism and its various institutional components is the best and most reliable way to advance and protect a polity that is democratic in spirit and substance. Accordingly, this bold and counter-intuitive stance towards a constitutionalist vision of democratic governance must be taken seriously:

> Constitutions generate a set of inviolable principles to which future law and government activity more generally must conform. This function ... is vital to the functioning of democracy. Without a commitment to higher law, the state operates for the short-term benefit of those in power or the current majority ... By limiting the scope of government and recommitting politicians to respect certain limits, constitutions make government possible.[5]

Perhaps the most compelling and celebrated effort to promote and bolster this constitutionalist approach to democracy has been made by the late Ronald Dworkin. Throughout his large body of work, Dworkin defended the jurisprudential position that a combination of constitutionalism and democracy is not only possible but also best exemplifies the special appeal of American politics and its historical practice. Making the very important point that democracy is not simply a procedural ideal, he insists that it also entails a commitment to certain substantive principles of political morality. As such, his favoured interpretation of the democratic ideal is "partnership democracy" that he distinguishes from a strictly procedural conception that he labels "majoritarian democracy." The majoritarian view maintains that democracy is simply government in accordance with the will of the greatest number of people as expressed in the election of officials. On this understanding, the policies adopted by a legislative assembly can be characterized as democratic because they are favoured by a majority of the electorate. But this view does not hold that the majority is always right or that its decisions will always be fair. On the contrary, a majority may make very wrong or unjust decisions, but that is not relevant for characterizing those decisions as democratic. For Dworkin's majoritarian, the question of democracy is exhausted in the procedure by which a decision is taken: substantive content is eclipsed by procedural source. As such, the majoritarian view of democracy "allows us to say ... that a decision is democratic even if it is very unjust" and, therefore, presents itself as a purely procedural ideal, independent of other dimensions of political morality.[6]

According to Dworkin, the obvious problem with this conception is that it cannot explain what is good about democracy because it incorrectly assumes that the sheer weight of popular numbers contributes something of special value to a political decision. In this respect, Dworkin claims that some of the traditional arguments in favour of majority rule (e.g., that majority rule results in wiser and better government and that it is the only fair method of decision-making) are mistaken. He maintains that there is no reason, historical or philosophical, to think that a majority is any more likely to reach the right answer about moral issues than a minority. Moreover, he contests the claim that majority rule is fair because it gives each citizen equal political power: representative government gives much more power over political decisions to people who hold office than people who do not. For Dworkin, therefore, the partnership view of democracy qualifies the relationship between majority rule and democracy. For him, democracy does not mean that the majority should always or even most of the time have the final word: all that democracy requires is that the people govern themselves by treating each individual as a full partner in a collective enterprise.[7] Consequently, in Dworkin's partnership version of democracy, decisions are democratic *only* when the conditions that protect the status and interests of each individual as a full partner are met. Thus, when a community decides by majority rule (or by close to unanimity for that matter) to ignore the interests of some individual or group, its decision will not simply be unjust and open to rebuke, it will have nothing to do with democracy.

Unlike the majoritarian view of democracy, partnership democracy not only has substantive implications but also is defended by Dworkin precisely because "democracy is a substantive, not a merely procedural ideal."[8] The merit of a particular law or policy and, therefore, its potential to improve democracy is not assessed by considering the procedure by which it came into being; its substantive cut and content must be consistent with and preferably capable of advancing the demands of equal partnership. If that theory allows for such content, then the law or policy has democratic credentials whether it would have arisen from majoritarian politics or not. In Dworkin's approach, therefore, the true test of democratic merit is less whether it has an appropriate institutional source or procedural pedigree in people's political views and more whether it is compatible with and can be made to square with the philosophical demands of Dworkin's two foundational principles of human dignity.

Nevertheless, Dworkin does consider that the partnership view of democracy has procedural implications. When there are disagreements about what law or policy is more consistent with a democratic ideal, there must be a reliable procedure in place for reaching collective decisions. Not surprisingly, as with the substantive implications of partnership democracy, these procedures must follow from the same principles of intrinsic value and personal responsibility. From the former, it can be deduced that a community must show equal concern for the human beings that live within its borders. According to Dworkin, this is best achieved with widespread and roughly equal suffrage because "officials elected by a broad swath of the population will do a much better job of protecting the weak against special privilege and tyranny than officials elected by and responsible to only a few":[9] the test of whether a constitutional arrangement shows genuine procedural equality is to inquire whether it produces outcomes that respect people's substantive equality.

Similarly, from the second principle of human dignity, Dworkin concludes that it follows that political arrangements must respect the personal responsibility of individuals. This is taken to imply that a contingent majority has no automatic right to impose its will over other human beings, even if the majority's laws and policies are designed in a way that further their overall interests. Consequently, the second principle of human dignity is considered to require that the basic procedure utilized to reach and validate collective decisions be compatible with the principle of self-government. Although it might compromise a person's dignity to submit to the decisions of others, such dignity is not compromised when that person does take part, as an equal partner, in those decisions. The upshot of this is that Dworkin understands the institutional implications of self-government primarily in terms of the protection of certain individual rights. While all persons must be able to participate in collective decisions, there are certain aspects of each participant's life that must not be susceptible to interference by such collective decisions. In this respect, therefore, the usual slate of fundamental rights must be guaranteed, including the right to participate in collective decisions as both voter and candidate for office. This will ensure that the majority will not impose its will in deciding whether and how, for example, religion or other ethical values will play a part in an individual's life.

By way of conclusion, Dworkin argues that his account of partnership democracy, unlike the majoritarian one, fits very well with the structure of the American constitution and presents its history in its very best light. As he states, "The list of constitutional rights in the United States Constitution, as these have been interpreted by American courts over recent decades, does a reasonably good job of identifying and protecting the political rights that flow from the two principles of dignity and converting those political rights into legal rights."[10] Of course, that does not mean the United States is a paragon of partnership democracy, even if its basic structure approximates to its liberal ideal. As Dworkin demonstrates, some of the concrete policies adopted by its legislature violate the substantive requirements of the principle of intrinsic value and the principle of personal responsibility. Nevertheless, Dworkin makes a resounding case for why the general structure and practices of American constitutional politics are so desirable and definitive: exceptional lapses from democratic grace merely serve to prove the general rule of constitutionalist integrity.

In crafting and defending his account in *Is Democracy Possible Here?* and other writings, Dworkin has left no doubt that not only are constitutionalism and democracy compatible but also that his vision of liberal constitutionalism is the best available compromise between the two. Indeed, he is clear that popular politics are an inferior mode of constitutional politics because it is important to put many matters of political morality outside the reach of popular political debate and disagreement. For him, it is simply axiomatic that "constitutional rights ... are not compromises of democracy, but rather attempts to guarantee it."[11] In such an arrangement, it is not only appropriate but necessary that courts act as a "forum of principle" and, by way of constitutional review, serve as the final authority on contested matters of political morality. If judges do this properly, they will offer a moral reading of the constitution which will "elaborate a coherent constitutional morality."[12] Dworkin insists that this is not a violation of democratic governance but a realization of the very highest and substantive ambitions of democratic politics.

A Canadian Take

The central notion of constitutionalism is, therefore, that, although government is established to serve popular interests, an elected government's powers must be constrained in its powers if it is to retain authority in exercising those powers on behalf of popular interests. As such, constitutions not only organize and distribute power, they place limits and constraints upon its exercise. In its predominantly liberal incarnation, there is a strong belief that there must be procedural and substantive limits placed on what policies the citizens can require or expect their political institutions to pursue. In this vision, democracy is not the only or, in a Dworkinian-style rendition, main process by which political justice is

constituted or achieved; it is merely instrumental to the preservation and expression of that goal. There is, of course, much debate
among constitutionalists about the nature and extent of these limitations. Some of the most common arrangements relied upon to
achieve such a balance of power and accountability include the
familiar notions of separation of powers, adherence to the Rule
of Law, constitutional supremacy, and, of course, the protection of
fundamental rights through judicial review.

Perhaps more than most, Canada is a country that has a continuing debate about its constitutional arrangements. This debate covers
not only the legal structure of such arrangements but also the process
by which such a structure can connect to the political debate for its
alteration. Although this leads to more than its fair share of national
angst, Canada has at least been obliged to attend to the legitimacy
and substance of the basic building blocks in its constitutional tool-
kit. Of course, at the heart of this contemporary debate is the persistent problem of French-speaking Quebec's continued relationship
with the rest of Canada. This takes many different shapes and forms,
but a pressing issue has always been under what conditions, if any,
can Quebec determine its own political fate by becoming independent? This brings to the fore a whole host of difficult and enduring
concepts and practices – democracy, sovereignty, self-determination,
federalism, the Rule of Law, and the protection of insular minorities.
Few constitutional challenges call so acutely into question the whole
issue of what constitutions are, where they are to be found, and how
they are to be given meaning.

In the 1990s, the Supreme Court of Canada was pushed reluctantly into the breach and required to provide its legal judgment
on whether and, if so, under what circumstances Quebec might be
able to secede unilaterally from Canada. The particular question
to be answered was straightforward – "under the Constitution of
Canada, can the National Assembly, legislature or government of
Quebec effect the secession of Quebec from Canada unilaterally?"
The decision of the Supreme Court strongly exhibits the dilemmas
that confront any theoretical efforts to give meaningful and legitimate practical content to constitutional law in a modern democracy. The Supreme Court offered a more sophisticated account

of the problem and its possible solutions than much of the then-existing jurisprudential reflection. In a manner of speaking, when the constitutional rubber hits the political road, what are the immediate and practical implications of an enduring commitment to a constitutionalist approach to governance and politics?

The Supreme Court decided that Quebec could not secede unilaterally. It held that any political desire to secede is constrained by and must be implemented in accordance with existing constitutional commitments. Its bottom line was that, if there was a clear democratic vote in favour of secession, the rest of Canada would be obliged to negotiate with Quebec over the terms of its withdrawal from the Canadian Confederation. In arriving at this decision, the Supreme Court sought to clarify the delicate interplay between law and politics in a democracy and its own role in that dynamic confrontation. It did this by seeking to balance constitutional rights and obligations with existing legal structures and political initiatives. For instance, it decided that, whereas the legal order of the constitution prevented unilateral acts and required collective action, what constitutes "a clear democratic vote" and "legitimate negotiations" was a political matter that fell outside the legal mandate of the courts. As a unanimous Supreme Court concluded, "the task of the Court has been to clarify the legal framework within which political decisions are to be taken 'under the Constitution' and not to usurp the prerogatives of the political forces that operate within that framework."[13]

In reaching its specific decision and justifying it generally, the Supreme Court's judgment resonates strongly with the themes and motifs of liberal constitutionalist thought. The Supreme Court began with the foundational notion that, while constitutional texts are primary, they do not exhaust the constitution; there is a tradition of constitutional practice that encompasses but is not exhausted by written documents and enactments. As such, it argued. that there is "an historical lineage" whose underlying principles "inform and sustain the constitutional text." These principles include "federalism, democracy, constitutionalism and the Rule of Law, and respect for minorities" and inform the overall structure of the constitutional rights and obligations in play.[14] Consequently, the Supreme

Court saw its task as being to elaborate the meaning of these essential interpretive considerations and to explain how they each can be balanced and integrated within a harmonious whole. In the particular case at hand, the Supreme Court spent much of its time developing the theoretical content of the principle of democracy, the practical effects of it, and, perhaps most importantly, how it sits comfortably with the rest of the constitutionalist compact. This is no small undertaking.

In its unanimous opinion, the Supreme Court begins by accepting that the general meaning and specific demands of the principle of democracy within a larger constitutional context are far from self-evident or universally accepted. While Anglo-Canadian constitutional history has tended to equate the democratic imperative with majority rule, it was viewed as consisting of much more than that. As such, the Supreme Court stated that it is not simply concerned with the process of government: there is a substantive dimension that cannot be overlooked. According to its extensive judgment, these substantive goals include "to name but a few, respect for the inherent dignity of the human person, commitment to social justice and equality, accommodation of a wide variety of beliefs, respect for cultural and group identity, and faith in social and political institutions which enhance the participation of individuals and groups in society."[15] However, the Supreme Court concedes that how those values are to be particularized and defined as well as how they interact is itself never fixed, but are instead part of the continuing debate over what democratic commitment entails: "a democratic system of government is committed to considering dissenting voices and seeking to acknowledge and address those voices in the laws by which all in the community must live."[16]

This broader and more nuanced understanding of democracy, of course, leads to an obvious difficulty – the two fundamental principles of procedural efficacy and substantive justice to which constitutional democracy is committed are, at worst, incompatible and, at best, in the most severe tension. According to one principle, the will of the citizens as expressed through the available political procedures should govern and any limits on this exercise of popular power are unjustifiable. But this principle competes with the other equally important principle. This holds that the majority cannot do whatever it likes in the name of democracy; there are certain outcomes that cannot be tolerated in a society that claims to be just, no matter how democratic the procedures that gave rise to them. For societies to be worthy of the label "democratic," there must be a balance between the procedural and substantive dimensions which, being contingent and contextual, will change and vary over time: "democracy is not simply concerned with the process of government, [but] ... is fundamentally connected to substantive goals."[17]

In order to operationalize this view of democracy as demanding more than majority rule, the Supreme Court recognizes that popular sovereignty has to be supplemented and constrained by other constitutional principles. For the Supreme Court, therefore, majority rule combines with other constitutional principles to ensure that democracy is implemented and respected in a procedural as well as substantive way:

> The consent of the governed is a value that is basic to our understanding of a free and democratic society. Yet democracy in any real sense of the word cannot exist without the Rule of Law. It is the law that creates the framework within which the "sovereign will" is to be ascertained and implemented. To be accorded legitimacy, democratic institutions must rest, ultimately, on a legal foundation. That is, they must allow for the participation of, and accountability to, the people, through public institutions created under the Constitution. Equally, however, a system of government cannot survive through adherence to the law alone. A political system must also possess legitimacy, and in our political culture, that requires an interaction between the Rule of Law and the democratic principle. The system must be capable of reflecting the aspirations of the people ...
>
> Constitutional government is necessarily predicated on the idea that the political representatives of the people of a province have the capacity and the power to commit the province to be bound into the future by the constitutional rules being adopted. These rules are "binding" not in the sense of frustrating the will of a majority of a province, but as defining the majority which must be consulted in order to alter the fundamental balances of political power (including the spheres of autonomy guaranteed by the principle of federalism), individual rights,

and minority rights in our society. Of course, those constitutional rules are themselves amenable to amendment, but only through a process of negotiation which ensures that there is an opportunity for the constitutionally defined rights of all the parties to be respected and reconciled. In this way, our belief in democracy may be harmonized with our belief in constitutionalism. Constitutional amendment often requires some form of substantial consensus precisely because the content of the underlying principles of our Constitution demand it. By requiring broad support in the form of an 'enhanced majority' to achieve constitutional change, the Constitution ensures that minority interests must be addressed before proposed changes which would affect them may be enacted.[18]

So expressed, the Supreme Court is adamant that majority rule is not tantamount to democracy and does not take precedence over all other values and principles in the Canadian constitutional order: "it is evident that our Constitution contemplates that Canada shall be a constitutional democracy: the representative and democratic nature of our political institutions was simply assumed." For the Supreme Court judges, any other argument is said to misunderstand in the most profound way the meaning of popular sovereignty and the nature of a constitutional democracy: "constitutionalism facilitates – indeed, makes possible – a democratic political system by creating an orderly framework within which people may make political decisions." Accordingly, in a similar call to constitutionalist arms as Dworkin and other liberal theorists, the Supreme Court places the commitment to democracy within a broader, if limiting constitutional framework and concludes that both reinforce, not undermine each other: "without that relationship, the political will upon which democratic decisions are taken would itself be undermined."[19] In short, democracy is the undeniable jewel in the constitutionalist crown.

A Judicial Aside

The main elements of most modern states' constitutional orders were firmly in place before all persons were treated as citizens and before the franchise was extended to all those citizens. Much has changed since then. Whereas the rise and thrust of constitutions were directed at putting a check on monarchical or aristocratic control, the present situation faces a very different challenge. The growth of democracy as both an idea and practice has raised pressing concerns for political and legal theorists. In particular, while the structures and details of constitutional orders have developed and changed over time, the challenge of increased popular participation has obliged a re-examination of the appropriate and legitimate relationship between constitutionalism and democracy.[20] In short, constitutionalist advocates have shifted their focus and targeted unchecked popular and democratic majorities as the main source of the actual threat to government stability and constitutional justice.

Although there is much to admire about both liberal theorists' and judicial supporters' efforts to defend and integrate the procedural and substantive elements of democracy within a broader constitutionalist framework, there remains the thorny and teasing question of how that balance is to be struck and by whom. The almost universal response has been to designate courts as the most desirable and best institution to perform that crucial and difficult task. Of course, this reliance on the judicial review of legislative and executive action has brought with it some obvious challenges about its legitimacy. This has been conveniently termed "the counter-majoritarian difficulty" – why should a small group of people (i.e., judicial bureaucrats) who are by design much less accountable to and much less representative of the public at large be entitled to pass constitutional judgment on and invalidate or curtail the important decisions and actions of a larger group of people (i.e., the legislature and executive arms of government) who are much more accountable and representative of the public at large?[21]

It should come as no surprise that legal theorists and constitutional jurists have had great trouble with making a cogent and compelling response to this challenge. Because of judges' problematic democratic status, it has become necessary to develop an interpretive method through which a sufficient gap can be maintained between their own political instincts and the contested values of the constitutional order. If judges are to resolve constitutional disputes when political actors are divided, they have to be able to do so in a way that is itself non-partisan. After all, constitutions are intended to be a higher law that provides a neutral and objective framework within which day-to-day politics can be conducted in a partisan and even ideological way. Consequently, because the constitution is supposed to be above the political fray and should itself have no particular political slant or orientation, those empowered to enforce it should be expected to do their work in an equally neutral and objective way; constitutional law must not be reducible to partisan politics. The effort to elucidate and defend such an approach to the constitutional responsibilities of courts in a democracy has been demanding and elusive: it goes to the heart of the constitutionalist ambition. Without such an explanation or account, the constitutionalist agenda and ambition will be fatally undermined.

The traditional answer to the constitutionalist dilemma was that judges applied pre-existing rules, but did not create those rules. If ever this stance was viable or convincing, it is no longer so. No self-respecting jurist defends judicial conduct in constitutional law on such entirely formalist terms. Today, there are a whole range of theories that claim to offer an account of what it is that judges do and should do in fulfilling their institutional role of interpreting and applying the Constitution in a democratic society.[22] They tend to look to the imperatives of formal objectivity and substantive justice: there is a felt need to provide some method or technique by which judges can give meaning to the Constitution that is both capable of giving substantive direction and consistency to decisions reached and that is itself not reducible to only their own (or an enabling jurist's) political and moral commitments. At the heart of these efforts is the audacious claim that it is judges' non-democratic status (i.e., being unaccountable and unrepresentative) that guarantees the institutional and intellectual detachment necessary to ensure fundamental and contested matters of political justice are addressed and resolved in an impartial and legal way. Judges are professional and principled; they are not merely crass politicians in robes. As such, they are better placed to protect democracy against its own excesses.

Whether by way of grand theorizing or through case-by-case criticisms, judges and jurists have sought to understand and handle the tensions between power and principle, politics and personnel, tradition and change, and much else besides in accounting for the performance and perils of constitutional adjudication. Some of the leading and most popular accounts on offer within the constitutionalist canon include the following:

- *Principlists* – Eschewing any faith in the idea that constitutional law was about simple rule-application, these jurists instead insist that a viable and attractive check on judges is to be found in the practice of principled adjudication. The challenge and promise of this way of proceeding is that, leaving the relative safety of a rule-based approach, the attendant fear of falling prey to "the *ad hoc* in politics" can be resisted by looking for principled grounds of normative reasoning that "in their generality and their neutrality transcend any immediate result that is involved."[23] This approach permits judges to enter the worlds of values, but to do so in a way that finesses the treacherous swamps of contested political values.
- *Moralists* – While accepting that a principled approach is essential, these adherents contend that this cannot be done in an entirely "general" or "neutral" way. For them, constitutional adjudication demands that judges make political and moral choices, but not of a partisan or personal kind. The law has its own political morality and it is for judges to identify it, develop it consistently, and apply it to the particular matter at hand.[24] Although this obliges judges to confront and negotiate the world of ideological contestation, this is a task that cannot and should not be shied away from. But, by making such choices in a principled and professionally mandated way, they can work the important tension between the law as it is and the law as it ought to be.
- *Originalists* – Unpersuaded that the moralist or principlist task can be completed without playing politics of the most basic and unmitigated kind, these jurists advocate a way of proceeding that recognizes that the Constitution had an objective and stable meaning when enacted and that this should govern judicial review going forward. Although there is much internal debate within the originalist camp about how that meaning is to be fixed and applied today, the predominant thrust is to give a substantive and practical

bite to the text's sweeping and abstract declarations by determining what they meant in that society at that time.[25] If people do not like the results of that adjudicative responsibility, then it is for politicians, not judges, to amend or update the Constitution.

- *Pragmatists* – Abandoning the grander and unattainable ambitions of both the moralists and originalists, these jurists reject not only on-the-fly *ad hoc* decision-making, but also any dogmatic allegiance to an overarching methodology. They hold that the work of judges is bounded by law, but not narrowly or legalistically so. Drawing upon an established and practical tradition of legal argumentation, judges must act in good faith and strive for reasoned justice under law; they should not stray too far from received notions of justice and common sense.[26] In all aspects of their judicial performance, judges must be self-consciously reasonable about the approach they adopt, the reasons that they give and the decisions that they reach.

- *Democratists* – Disenchanted by what they consider to be disingenuous traditional efforts to confront the counter-majoritarian dilemma, these jurists insist that the only way that courts can act legitimately is by being inspired directly by the goals and ambitions of democracy itself. Accordingly, they recommend that judges must only and always act to ensure that representative channels of democracy are kept open so as to close the gap between citizens and their representatives.[27] As such, judges gain political legitimacy as well as constitutional guidance from seeking to give expression to the marginalized and excluded voices of the people in contributing to the ideological debates that shape government policy and practice.

Accordingly, each of these approaches seeks to make good on the obvious democratic deficit that is created by giving unelected judges the duty to interpret and apply the Constitution to the actions of elected representatives or public officials. At bottom, the theoretical and practical conceit is that, although judges might appear to be undemocratic (or, at least, non-democratic) in status and performance, they are better and more reliable defenders and promoters of democratic governance than anyone else. It is their very detached and professional nature that underwrites their democratic legitimacy and commitment: they can engage with ideological politics, but not be consumed or captured by it. Of course, some judges will fall short of constitutionalism's supposed exacting standards, but this will not be sufficient to impugn the whole judicial enterprise. Moreover, efforts to diversify the judiciary and render its appointments more amenable to democratic control are to be applauded, but they are not essential for constitutionalists if judges act appropriately and professionally in fulfilling their constitutional duties. As such, therefore, a commitment to a constitutionalist-empowered and -limited judiciary, as the Canadian Supreme Court put it, "facilitates – indeed, makes possible – a democratic political system."[28]

Conclusion

As showcased and celebrated by its proponents, constitutionalism has much to offer and recommend it. Yet, as with almost every theoretical account, there is a dark side as well as a bright one to the constitutionalist road. In particular, constitutionalism defends a vision of governance in which fixed and strong constitutional arrangements take precedence over the dynamism of democratic politics. Indeed, it is the very unpredictability and unruliness of those politics that gives rise to the controlling and elitist nature of constitutionalism. Consequently, constitutionalism is also characterized by an obsession with permanence, a resistance to constitutional change, and a suspicion of constituent assemblies. Underlying many constitutionalist theories is the idea that, once the constitution contains the right abstract principles and the correct balance of institutional safeguards, it is a good and finished constitution. There is room for fine-tuning in the details of its operation and implementation as circumstances change, but there is no need or warrant for further changes of a substantial or structural kind. Indeed, the claim is that to alter the constitutional arrangements in significant ways is to look for political trouble to play with the stability of the governance system, and to risk the precious ideal of the Rule of Law.[29]

chapter three

Constitutional Origins: Undemocratic Beginnings?

Few events are as shrouded in myth as the founding of nations and their natal constitutional arrangements; they are bequeathed as occasions of erasure and forgetting. It seems a central part of the national psyche that those origins should be definitive in nature and noble in ambition. In some circumstances, those stories of national creation might be uplifting and entirely warranted: in others, it might be more of an exercise in ideological window-dressing. On many occasions, the truth lies somewhere between the two. Yet it does seem significant to address the historical circumstances and socio-political conditions in which a nation was born and the role that a constitution played in that initial process. That being said, it is not so far-fetched to consider that the founding context might well be indicative of the extent to which the constitution deserves to be taken seriously as an arrangement that reflects and embodies a set of values that accounted for the genuine motivations and political agendas of its founders. In particular, the setting for constitutional formation might reveal much about the relationship between constitutionalist sentiments and democratic realities.

In this chapter, therefore, I intend to look at the historical context of the formation of the American and Canadian nations and their constitutional structures. This is a daunting, if revealing exercise. While there is now a marked tendency to view these origins and their participants as almost sacred in design and performance, they amounted to "a messy moment populated by mere mortals, whose chief task was to fashion a series of artful political compromises."[1]

First, I take a more realistic look at the circumstances and conditions in which the American Constitution was conceived and drafted; it was an occasion of much democratic trumpeting, but little democratic participation. The second section examines the later creation of the Canadian constitutional scheme; while the founders are less revered than their American counterparts, they are still considered to be as elevated a group as Canadian history allows. Thirdly, I explore the democratic dynamics of the so-called repatriation of the Canadian Constitution in 1982 and the addition of a Charter of Rights and Freedoms; this formative era was no less political and pragmatic than any other. Finally, I take issue with the accepted reliance upon so-called unwritten constitutional principles to supplement and inform the primary written resources of the constitutional regime. Throughout, the emphasis is upon the dubious democratic pedigree of constitutions in both their written and unwritten dimensions.

An American Experiment

The United States Constitution is now almost 220 years old. It is the oldest constitution in the world. While there have been twenty-seven formal amendments (the first ten of which occurred in 1791 and comprise the Bill of Rights), it stands as the basic and fundamental instrument for allocating and limiting governmental power and authority. This means that the United States' basic scheme of government is very much anchored in the circumstances and concerns of the late eighteenth century. This, of course, is a blessing and a blight. Although many celebrate its longevity and permanence as signs of its ageless wisdom and enduring appeal, others are troubled by its origins in a time that bears little or no relevance to contemporary conditions and challenges. Nevertheless, no matter how you look at it, the Constitution did not arise in the most democratic of circumstances or conditions. The question, therefore, is to what extent those circumstances influence and infiltrate its later history and present democratic appeal.

Americans tend to look back with nostalgic pride at the efforts and ambitions of the so-called Founding Fathers. In contrast to present-day politics, it is seen to be a vaunted era when high-minded and public-spirited political leaders set aside their petty political differences and rose to the challenge of drafting a blue-print for a lasting and just republican society. This roseate depiction masks as much as it reveals. After all, ten of the first twelve presidents owned some slaves and so did two of the earliest chief justices. Although the basic facts about the creation of the Constitution are a matter of trite learning (and so need little rehearsal), there are matters that need to be revisited and emphasized in order to give a more sober account. In short, despite the soaring rhetoric and noble posturing, the overall constitution-making event was a thoroughly elitist enterprise in its personnel and purposes that was motivated by distinctly parochial concerns. More tellingly, it had almost nothing to do with democracy at all.

On 25 May 1787, the Constitutional Convention opened in Phil-adelphia with fifty-five delegates who, being merchants, bank-ers, lawyers, and well-heeled farmers, were the educated elite of American society; they had mainly served as colonial or state legislators and were largely Protestant in religious allegiance. The delegates represented twelve of the thirteen states that then made up the United States. The exception was Rhode Island. For reasons that went to the heart of the matter, Rhode Island had decided not to take part because it was averse to establishing a powerful federal government that would likely interfere in its economy and local business. This underlying issue informed and shaped much of the political wrangling that characterized the Convention. Indeed, the Convention sessions were held in private, without reporters or other observers, in order to allow delegates to speak candidly, negotiate openly, and compromise freely; this was not exactly a democratic process in practice or purpose. Moreover, the delegates were not creating a constitu-tion from scratch; considerable attention was paid to customary understanding and practices about the most efficient and effica-cious ways of organizing government as understood in a late eighteenth-century context.

The resulting constitutional accord was brought forward for a final vote on 17 September 1787. Although a grandiloquently crafted document – "We the People of the United States, in Order to form a more perfect Union, establish Justice, insure domestic Tranquility, provide for the common defence, promote the general Welfare, and secure the Blessings of Liberty to ourselves and our Posterity" – it represented a set of makeshift resolutions and compromises. These conciliations were necessary in order to obtain and maintain the support of a majority of delegates. By the time of the final vote, some delegates had already abandoned the enterprise and even some who remained refused to sign the proposed Constitution. Out of the original fifty-five, only thirty-nine delegates supported and signed the final proposal. Indeed, in his final summation to the Convention, Benjamin Franklin struck a suitably resigned and pragmatic tone. He did not so much laud its grandeur and ideal character as make a political plea for its contingent adequacy and immediate timeliness:

> I confess that there are several parts of this constitution which I do not at present approve, but I am not sure I shall never approve them … I agree to this Constitution with all its faults … I doubt too whether any other Convention we can obtain, may be able to make a better Constitution. For when you assemble a number of men to have the advantage of their joint wisdom, you inevitably assemble with those men, all their prejudices, their passions, their errors of opinion, their local interests, and their selfish views. From such an assembly can a perfect production be expected? … Thus I consent, Sir, to this Constitution because I expect no better, and because I am not sure, that it is not the best … If every one of us in returning to our Constituents were to report the objections he has had to it, … we might prevent its being generally received, and thereby lose all the salutary effects and great advantages resulting naturally in our favor among foreign Nations as well as among ourselves, from our real or apparent unanimity … I cannot help expressing a wish that every member of the Convention who may still have objections to it, would with me, on this occasion doubt a little of his own infallibility, and to make manifest our unanimity, put his name to this instrument.[2]

Franklin's exhortation was successful and the Constitution was forwarded on for approval by the Congress of the Confederation in New York. Amid contested and heated debate, the Congress took the unusual, but savvy step of passing a unanimous resolution to submit the document to the states for ratification, without confirming whether they were for or against it. There followed a period of intense disputation between the opposing anti-Federalists and the supporting Federalists; this gave rise to a rich and partisan parsing of the Constitution's content and clauses. In September 1788, the Congress voted to adopt the new Constitution with eleven of the states on board; it was to come into effect on 4 March 1789. Over the next twenty months or so, the other two states, North Carolina and Rhode Island, came into line and ratified the Constitution; they were the subject of strong-arm tactics. In 1789, James Madison, as a new member of the House of Representatives, introduced nineteen amendments to the Constitution. Congress accepted twelve of them and sought the states' ratification. Ten of these amendments were approved: these came to be the Bill of Rights and became part of the Constitution on 10 December 1791.[3]

Throughout the process, there was no popular vote or referendum on the adoption of the new Constitution. This lack of any popular imprimatur on the Constitution's substance and adoption should come as no surprise. Apart from the whole process being designed and dominated by the political elite, the state of democracy was truly limited and woeful at the time. There was no mention at all of "democracy" in the Declaration of Independence or the Constitution. As regards eligibility to vote, a very small portion of the overall population was enfranchised. It included only property-owning or tax-paying white males; this amounted to about 6 per cent of the overall population. But the capacity to vote was the least of the problems for most people. Women, Black persons, Indigenous people, and more than half of white men were not only disenfranchised but also disempowered generally in a hierarchical and oppressive society.[4] Of course, a large bulk of the population was actually enslaved. Indeed, the Philadelphia Convention had not taken seriously the idea of abolishing slavery. The Southern states were adamant that the legality of slavery should be left to individual states and the Northern states acceded to this as a condition of there being any Union or Constitution at all. Consequently, any claim to there being a genuine democratic ambition or popular source to the constitutional bargains made it almost impossible to sustain.

Accordingly, the Constitution of the United States was conceived and created not only in a society of widespread discrimination and gross inequality but also by an elite group of white men who paid little regard to that extant state of affairs. Talk of "all men being created equal" and "We the People" was simply so much rhetoric and posturing. There never was any serious intention or desire to live up to those grandiloquent aspirations. While the American Founding Fathers were men of their time and not much different to their global colleagues, they did present their new constitutional arrangements and commitments as being the dawning of a new and just compact between government and its citizens. This was a canard. The fact that they might have believed their own propaganda (and that is entirely debatable) did not mean that later generations could or should do the same. The new Constitution was about consolidating traditional elite bases of power: reference to any democratic ideal was conspicuous by its absence and, at best, an afterthought.

There have, of course, been amendments to the Constitution since 1789. The process of amendment is cumbersome and decidedly so. In general, it requires a two-thirds majority in both parts of Congress and ratification by two-thirds of the states.[5] In the intervening 230 years or so, over 11,539 proposals to amend the Constitution have been made to Congress. Out of those, thirty-three have been passed by Congress and sent for approval by the States; the last one was in 1992. As will be obvious, this process remains very much about governmental action as opposed to popular initiative. While the democratic status of elected politicians had improved as the extent of the franchise was broadened, the actual involvement of ordinary people was indirect and largely inconsequential. Moreover, under Article V of the Constitution, there is also the possibility of there being called into play a national convention for the purpose of amendment. This was intended to be similar to the original convention of 1787; it would comprise elected and representative persons from the wider body politic. While this would have had a more democratic pedigree than the more general amendment process, no such convention has ever actually been constituted, even though there have been many calls for such an institution to be created and utilized.

A Canadian Occasion

It was not until about seventy-five years or so after the American constitutional experience that Canada confronted its own challenges of becoming a (colonial) nation and creating its own constitutional scheme of governance. Still under the considerable control and tutelage of the British Parliament, the founding documents of the new Canadian polity were the product of a small coterie of colonial politicians and businessmen from Ottawa and London. Brokered as much as born, the creation of modern-day Canada was effected by the British North America Act of 1867. It resulted from protracted and angry negotiations between the existing provinces – Ontario (Lower Canada), Quebec (Upper Canada), New Brunswick, and Nova Scotia. Against strong provincial opposition, a delegation of fifteen was sent to London and, in consultation with the Colonial Office of the British government, it cobbled together an elaborate, but far from exhaustive set of provisions that was acceptable to interested parties and provinces. In particular, it was resolved to keep Canada as part of the British Commonwealth and to retain the monarch as the head of state (as it is to this day). The ensuing act was given royal assent by Queen Victoria in March 1867 and Canada became a nation on 1 July 1867. Negotiations to embrace other provinces continued for a further nine years until 1873 when the last founding province agreed to join the federation.

The British North America Act sets the tone and substance of Canadian constitutionalism with its preamble – "a Constitution similar in Principle to that of the United Kingdom."[6] The act limits itself to allocating and distributing power among the different institutions of government and maps the respective powers of the federal and provincial governments. There was no equivalent to the American Bill of Rights. This was not because such rights, even in their attenuated and privileged form, were not considered important, but because it was simply assumed that Canadian citizens would receive the unwritten and entrenched rights of British citizens; those included fair trials, religious freedom, freedom of assembly, and the like. There was no need for any ratification of the act in Canada as it was an enactment of the British Parliament and did not depend upon the assent of the federal and provincial legislatures or its constituents. The only vaguely democratic dimension of this nation-building exercise was that the British Parliament was ultimately answerable to the narrow and, from a Canadian standpoint, indirect British electorate.

By 1867, democracy had begun to gain more traction in Canada as a political ideal and practice than it did at the time of the creation of the American constitutional regime. However, it still played an entirely lesser role in the country's first step to national status than might be thought. Canada's soon-to-be first prime minister and the main driving force towards Confederation, John A. Macdonald, had little tolerance for the idea of there being any basic right for ordinary people to participate or vote on proposals. As he bluntly put it, "As it would be obviously absurd to submit the complicated details of such a measure to the people, it is not proposed to seek their sanction before asking the Imperial Government to introduce a Bill in the British Parliament."[7] Against such a background, the American approach seemed positively democratic in spirit and process. While the popular vote in American presidential elections had risen by the mid-1860s to a meagre 15 per cent of the total population (although women and most Black people still could not vote even after the Civil War and general emancipation), the popular vote in Canada was almost half that. The franchise was restricted to adult white men who were British subjects and who owned a certain amount of property. This meant that, in broad terms, only about 360,000 people were eligible to vote out of a population of about 3.2 million; the relatively large number of Indigenous people (around 125,000) was simply ignored. Indeed, in the 1867 election, there was a voter turnout of about 268,000: this amounted to about 8 per cent of the total population. To suggest that this represented any kind of genuinely democratic process or practice is fanciful.

Canadians had to wait another 115 years until 1982 for the establishment of a full and home-grown Constitution. Although this so-called patriation process had a more democratic character and pedigree than its 1867 predecessor, it was by and large still a similarly elite and imposed affair. Elected on an unspecified mandate, national politicians bickered and bargained over the terms and conditions of any proposed constitutional changes; political paybacks, ideological resentments, local antagonisms, and personal egos fuelled a protracted and bitter chapter in the country's continuing national saga. Although not quite as romanticized as the American constitutional process of nation-making in 1787, the patriation of the Canadian Constitution has since been characterized as a cathartic expression of national unity and maturity. In fact, the so-called people's package of 1982 was hardly ever little more than a shrewd series of political accommodations by partisan leaders that did as much to perpetuate old antipathies, particularly between Quebec and the rest of Canada, and generate future bad political blood for good measure.[8] The role of popular participation in the overall decision-making process was defined by its almost complete absence. There was no broad national coming-together or spirit of solidarity; it was a largely political deal that was somehow transformed into a constitutional compact of almost mythical proportions.

A People's Package?

Since 1867, there have been a number of formal changes to the Canadian Constitution. As Canada has developed and grown, there was a more extensive cutting of the ties to the United Kingdom and the commonwealth. Various amendments and understandings were made with the approval of the British legislature. In particular, appeals from the Supreme Court of Canada to the Judicial Committee of the House of Lords were abandoned in 1949.

Also, legislative initiatives were completed by the federal government and provinces alike to introduce human rights schemes that
would bind them in exercising their constitutionally designated
functions. Simultaneously, in the common-law spirit of the British
Constitution, the Canadian Constitution adapted itself informally
to changing historical circumstances and social conditions; new
doctrines and conventional rules were shaped and followed. However, at the end of the 1970s, a confluence of political forces came
into being that pointed towards a shift away from a more British
Burkean tradition in constitutional matters to a more American
Lockean stance. The patriation of the Constitution would also give
rise to a different kind of Canadian approach to constitutionalism.

The process of constitutional patriation was almost entirely
elitist and non-democratic in shape and style. Although making gestures towards the importance of democracy as a bedrock
issue in Canadian politics, there was no formal role for the voices
and views of the Canadian people: no elections were held and
no referenda took place on the constitutional issue. In particular,
Indigenous people (who were not fully enfranchised until 1960)
remained entirely outside the process. Political leaders saw themselves as legitimately and best placed to re-engineer the constitutional structure and make it more conducive to advancing and
protecting the interests of ordinary Canadians. For them, democracy was as much about enshrining rights and freedoms and placing them beyond the reach of representative institutions as it was
about facilitating popular participation. Indeed, as was the case
in 1789 in the United States and 1867 in Canada, the notion of
"popular sovereignty" was deployed as a cover to maintain rule
by the established political and economic elites. Although a resort
to democratic involvement was mooted, it was done as much as a
political and bargaining threat as a genuine desire to seek popular
approval for broad-ranging and influential constitutional changes.
The whole cast of players were white, male, and middle-aged.

The motivating vision for Canada's new constitutional order was
very much that of Pierre Trudeau (and father of Justin Trudeau, the
current prime minister). A law professor by background and a political firebrand by instinct, he made the patriation of the constitution,

along with an entrenched bill of rights, his personal and national mission. He had made some modest efforts to achieve this in his earlier spell as prime minister in the mid-1970s. But, on returning to power in February 1980 and with a 60 per cent federalist victory in the Quebec separatist referendum in May, the time seemed ripe to bring his constitutional plans to fruition. Initial efforts were made to bring the provinces on board. Although there was some provincial support, the majority were opposed to the introduction of a charter of rights. In response, Trudeau's Liberal government threatened to go it alone by approaching the British government directly and by holding a federal referendum. At this point, the action moved out of the political arena and into the legal arena. If a deal concocted by political leaders lacked substantial democratic legitimacy, a court-dominated one was even less appealing.

After the British government indicated in January 1981 that it might not rubber-stamp a contested unilateral approach by the federal government, a reference was made to the Supreme Court of Canada about the constitutionality of such a move. In September, it was decided that, although there was no legal obstacle to the federal government proceeding unilaterally, there had developed a constitutional convention that it should seek a substantial degree of provincial consent before doing so. Caught between a legal rock and a political hard place, the federal government went back to the provinces for one more political roll of the constitutional dice. When there seemed a real impasse to progress, a pivotal event occurred – there was a behind-closed-doors meeting between the provincial attorneys general and the federal minister of justice. A deal was brokered to include a Charter of Rights and Freedoms on the condition that a clause be included in the new Constitution that would provide for a "notwithstanding" or override power by which either federal or provincial governments could make a piece of legislation exempt from Charter scrutiny. There can be no doubt that, without such a provision, the constitutional log-jam would not have been broken.

Throughout this protracted and antagonistic process, the position of the separatist-controlled Quebec, as with so much in Canadian history, was critical. Its leader, René Lévesque, was as charismatic and as much a hard-liner as Pierre Trudeau, albeit with consistently opposite views. Quebec withheld its consent to the constitutional accord reached. French-speaking Quebec maintained that its heritage and aspirations as a distinct cultural and political entity within Canada had been sabotaged. The new version of federalism contained in the Constitution – an entirely Canadian amending formula, a Charter of Rights and Freedoms, a strengthened Supreme Court as final arbiter of constitutional disputes, increased provincial authority over natural resources, the recognition of Aboriginal peoples, and an override provision[9] – would be adverse to Quebec's self-understood interests. Accordingly, Quebec refused to go along with the patriation package. When the Constitution Act was accepted by the British Parliament and proclaimed by Queen Elizabeth II on 17 April 1982, Quebec refused to accept the legitimacy of the patriation and did not sign the new Constitution. Although there have been efforts to bring Quebec formally into the constitutional fold, this has still not been formally achieved: Quebec is fully bound by the terms of the newly patriated constitution, but it is not a signatory to it.[10]

Accordingly, it can be fairly reported that democracy had little or any role in the patriation of the Canadian Constitution in 1982. If anything, it can be concluded that the patriated constitution did much to neutralize any gains that had been made to give "popular sovereignty" any real teeth or political bite. Surprisingly, it was no more and perhaps less democratic than its American counterpart over more than 200 years earlier. Up to 1982, great steps forward had been made in Canada to ensure that the democratic rights and entitlements of all Canadians were addressed. Although there was clearly much work still to be done, it is simply wrong to assume that it was only with the introduction of the Charter of Rights and Freedoms (the Charter) that Canadians became full citizens. There was already a welfare state in place and citizens' rights were decently protected. Indeed, arguments can be made that the Charter has stymied the growth of certain individual rights and collective benefits, especially of a socio-economic kind. It is not so much that the Charter has not protected people's rights, but that it has limited their range and inhibited their recognition.[11] Furthermore, it has undoubtedly frustrated greater popular participation and relegated it to the margins of political activity and engagement: the detached Supreme Court has become the focal point of democratic politics.

The idea that the new Constitution was a "people's package," therefore, is bogus in both substantive and procedural terms. No effort was made to solicit popular views or seek people's collective approval. Although the politicians and leaders were of course democratically elected, the negotiations and deal-making had an executive momentum and dynamic of their own making. The effect of the new Constitution was to place matters that were previously in the political and democratic realm out of the reach of popular control and participation. Indeed, some might contend that this was the real purpose of the constitutional exercise. The inclusion of an "override" provision in the new Constitution offered some hope of a continuing reliance on parliamentary democracy (and, in that sense, was to be applauded). However, its use and the subsequent criticism of it as somehow illegitimate has meant that the provision has fallen into disuse. As such, the main democratic feature of the new constitutional order has been sidelined.[12] Created through a tenuous democratic process, the Constitution Act has become a document of selective and varying application. As the Supreme Court phrased it, "With the adoption of the Charter, the Canadian system of government was transformed to a significant extent from a system of Parliamentary supremacy to one of constitutional supremacy."[13]

The Unwritten Constitution

The main attention in constitutional history has been given to the written constitutional documents of 1789 in the United States and of 1867 and 1982 in Canada. Indeed, the uninformed observer could be forgiven for thinking that these were, if not the exclusive location of a country's constitution, at least the most authoritative and primary sources. However, many constitutionalists contend that they are only one source of the constitution's meaning and, at times, not the most binding or privileged resource in the over-all constitutional scheme of things. A constitution includes those usages, conventions, customs, statutes and other legal principles that are recognized as having constitutional force and effect – the Rule of Law, executive privilege, separation of powers, and even democratic accountability itself. Although this will come as a sur-prise to many citizens, this state of affairs is defended by most constitutionalists as being very much in line with the institutional demands and designs of a constitutional democracy. Indeed, in the United Kingdom, until very recently, its constitutional structure and substance was entirely unwritten and informal; there was no single set of textual sources to ground its basic political arrange-ments and protections for citizens.

In the United States during the twentieth century, it became an accepted tenet of the constitutionalist credo that the constitu-tional text does not exhaust the basic content and parameters of the nation's constitution. Although the formal text is treated as the primary and predominant focus of attention and authority, it is not considered to be the sole or exclusive source of constitutional con-tent. A range of scholars argue that a proper and full understand-ing of the American constitution must incorporate and account for a large body of sources – judicial precedents, long-standing traditions, governmental conventions, juristic texts, venerated speeches, and the like – that are legitimate and necessary sources for supplementing and making sense of the written Constitution.[14] Within the constitutionalist fold, while the nature and meaning of these sources remains vague and protean, this recognition of such unwritten or invisible principles is treated as being almost self-evident and incontestable. Of course, the Supreme Court's own privileged authority to give final and authoritative meaning to the Constitution, written and unwritten, is based on such an informal recognition of non-textual sources (in that instance, a judicial deci-sion of its own).[15]

Much the same process and recognition has occurred in Can-ada. It has long been accepted that the Canadian Constitution comprises a range of sources that have not been reduced to one codified document. Up to 1982, it was almost universally accepted that, in line with the British North America Act's preamble that the Canadian Constitution was supposed to be "a constitution similar in principle to that of the United Kingdom," the development of general standards and even the recognition of certain fundamental rights could and should be developed by the courts. With the enactment of the Constitution Act in 1982, much greater swathes of the Constitution were reduced into writing, including the Charter of Rights. Nevertheless, the existing and largely British common-law approach persisted and it was largely accepted that there were continuing sources of conventions and prerogatives that filled out the constitutional arsenal. Indeed, in its (in)famous decision in the Quebec Reference case of 1998, the Supreme Court laid out the scope and nature of such unwritten principles that included federalism, protection of minorities, judicial independence, and the like. For a short period, the Supreme Court even suggested that these unwritten principles might be used not only as interpretive aids and supplemental precepts, but also as a direct means to invalidate legislative or executive action. However, it soon backed off such an aggressive stance.[16]

The problem with this constitutionalist-approved initiative is clear from a democratic point of view – the origins of unwritten principles are not directly democratic even when understood by the weak democratic standards of written constitutions' origins. There is no popular input by way of either debate or acceptance; ordinary citizens play no part at all in bringing these principles into the constitutional fold and imbuing them with favoured institutional force. It is entirely up to judges to identify, validate, incorporate, and interpret these unwritten supplements to the written components of the overall Constitution. Of course, it might be contended that such unwritten principles are embedded in the democratic fabric of society and are then simply teased out by judges. This explanation represents judges as being mere conduits who simply and passively recognize the deeper commitments and traditions of the citizenry at large. Even if this was an accurate depiction of unwritten principles' origins (and I insist that it is not), it would still fail to satisfy any genuine norm of democratic validity. Although passed off as being neutral and objective in origin and effect, such unwritten principles do not pass democratic muster. Although judges claim to be acting independently and apolitically, they are relying upon a set of constitutional principles that they themselves have brought to life and institutionalized. In such circumstances and mindful that these unwritten principles are beyond the reach of ordinary democratic politics, there is little than can be considered to be democratic about the origin of constitutional principles and their application.[17] All of this is less about forgetting and more about not remembering in the first place.

Conclusion

Although the Constitutions of Canada and the United States are presented as the almost sacrosanct symbols of advanced democracy, they are less democratic in their origins than constitutionalists and many others would have people believe or admit to themselves. Although offered as something beyond and over day-to-day politics, they are very much a product of the political dynamics in play at their creation. Constitutions are not the Moses-like stone tablets that they are touted to be. Although said about the Canadian Constitution Act of 1982, this assessment of repatriation has a general salience to the whole constitution-making and amendment process – "the precarious result of a byzantine process in which accidents, personality, skill and sheer will-power were central to the final outcome."[18] Although claimed to be done in the name of democracy and in the cause of democratic enhancement, the Canadian and American Constitutions place democracy in the service of other and often non-democratic values and visions. As such, they embody a long-standing and deep commitment to strong constitutionalism over strong democracy.

chapter four

A Higher Justice:
Some Fundamental Problems

A central tenet of constitutionalist orthodoxy is that constitutions are supposed to stand above the political fray of regular ideological contestation. Within this view, it is accepted that constitutions are based on values, but that those values are so fundamental and so foundational that they merit an elevated or higher status in a society's structure and substantive commitments. Indeed, with more than a little whiff of religious fervour, one celebrated advocate of constitutionalism insisted that it was to be understood as "a belief in a constitutional order based on transcendent justice."[1] Traditionally, this has meant that certain values and principles were considered to have an enduring and almost other-worldly quality that any self-respecting society that aspired to be just and fair had to embody and live by. In its more modern guise, therefore, constitutionalism is not considered a hedge against autocratic or aristocratic rule. Its target is the so-called excesses of democratic rule – people cannot be trusted to do the right thing and not pander to their own more base and less reasonable instincts; the political process must be controlled and disciplined in case they overstep the limits of their capacities for lasting justice. Of course, at their most idealistic, such constitutionalists offer reassurance that such a stance is warranted in the name of democracy itself. These claims are very much attended and celebrated with the nervous laughter of angelic voices.

Accordingly, in this chapter, I want to explore what these particular values are as judged by constitutional documents and to ascertain whether they live up to the higher and uncontroversial status that their defenders claim for them. It will come as no surprise to learn that I maintain this is simply not so even on the face of constitutional documents, let alone in their practical interpretation and enforcement. While the general values contained in constitutions are mostly valuable and worthy of protection, they are skewed and selective in their content and scope. It is not so much what is in constitutions that is the problem, but what is not in them; the absence of certain commitments serves to underline the political partiality of those values that are in constitutions. After introducing the idea of fundamentality and looking at its pitfalls, I look at those rights and powers that have been included in the Canadian and American Constitutions to appreciate their partial and political nature. The next section looks at the public/private divide and considers the ideological effects of approaching the abuse of power through such a dichotomous lens. Finally, I summarize how the courts have contributed to the problem of fundamentality and the role that they have assumed in giving practical effect to the Constitutions' vague promises.

Into the Transcendent?

It has been a marked feature of the Anglo-American tradition of rational philosophical inquiry to insist that there are certain natural or inalienable rights that individuals possess as individuals that need no confirmation or enactment by states or governments. Although there is heated disagreement over both the provenance of such entitlements (e.g., religious revelation or *a priori* philosophical analysis) and the content of such rights (e.g., liberty or equality), there is a shared and almost unquestioning collective acceptance that people have certain claims to just treatment that transcend the nature and origins of any scheme of governance. Constitutionalists build and rely on this important assumption. As such, constitutions are not considered to be the source of such rights, but are more conceived to be an acknowledgment and affirmation of such sources and claims. In this sense, a constitution can be understood as a matter of higher law. Indeed, the United States' Declaration of Independence in 1776 begins with a ringing endorsement of the idea that "we hold these truths to be self-evident, that all men are created equal, that they are endowed by their Creator with certain inalienable rights."

This transcendental tendency was given a more recent theoretical twist and intellectual prestige by the political theorist Francis Fukuyama. As a matter of historical record, he claimed to document and defend a coherent and universal "History of Humankind" that inexorably and inevitably leads to the establishment of liberal democracy and its commitment to individual rights: "at the end of history, there are no serious ideological competitors ... [and] the end point of mankind's ideological evolution is the universalization of Western liberal democracy as the final form of human government." This extravagant claim received strong if fleeting praise within the constitutionalist community. Indeed, Fukuyama contrives to insist (in light of almost overwhelming social and historical evidence to the contrary) that, through an adherence to such fundamental values, "America's social and ethnic structures have been sufficiently fluid to prevent the emergence of rigid social classes, significant sub-nationalisms, and linguistic minorities."[2] Such bald assertions are as outrageous as they are wrong.

Although less doctrinaire and grandiose in scope than Fukuyama, constitutionalists have built on similar theoretical foundations in insisting that constitutional rights are not simply the product of contingent political agreements, but are the stuff of a higher and more transcendent process. Moreover, in the constitutionalists' eyes, if understood properly and taken seriously, the development and protection of these rights and entitlements will underwrite the achievement of social and political justice. For them, constitutional law and adjudication are or should be entirely insulated from normal political wrangling and debate. Instead, such constitutionalist practices inhabit a world of moral truths and ethical imperatives that place constitutional rights in a very different dimension of inquiry and validation – they are fundamental and, therefore, are capable of non-ideological articulation and resolution.[3] Of course, they recognize that there have been many periodic falls from constitutionalist grace, but they insist that this possibility of judges fulfilling their constitutional responsibilities in such a principled and impartial fashion is genuine and foundational. In this way, the mundane acts of the judiciary can be vouchsafed by a celebrated and defensible tradition of detached rational method that is separate from the messy and compromised world of normal politics.

The importance for the judiciary of treating those rights that are contained in the Constitution, whether express or implied, as having a fundamental character is twofold. One is that, by imbuing them with the aura of fundamentality, those rights are themselves viewed as non-political in the sense that they are beyond the realm of political contestation. Of course, many seek to perform such an ideological manipulation. The response of the courts is that, while some disagreement about the nature and reach of those rights is inevitable, the fundamental nature of those rights, when properly understood, is amenable to rational and neutral analysis, not merely political interpretation and ideological appropriation. However, the fact that constitutional rights are treated as fundamental does not mean that they are absolute in delineation and application. Courts concede that even fundamental rights are not self-defining or self-executing. Although resorting to other values and purposes will be inevitable, that process of elaboration and defence can also be done in a rational and neutral manner that does not require that judges swim in the treacherous waters of ideological disputation.

The second effect of designating constitutional rights as fundamental builds on this first consideration. If constitutional rights did not possess this fundamental character, the task of the courts would be infinitely more problematic than it already is. Beginning with an ostensible non-political base, the courts can at least claim to be doing their job from a starting-point that is neither partisan nor opportunistic. Without this initial premise, the courts' work would be little more than an ideological free-for-all. In entering the world of ideological dispute, the courts would be compromised from the word "go." Judges would have no way to distinguish their principled legal efforts from the political machinations of their governmental or executive colleagues in governance. Consequently, the characterization of constitutional rights as being fundamental is an essential first step in being able to defend any claim that judicial power can be exercised legitimately in a society that adheres to the importance of democracy as an authoritative standard for political action and accountability.

Indeed, the courts have made frequent reference to this idea that constitutional rights are fundamental and, as such, can be used to discipline the legislative and executive branches of government when their acts and efforts fall short of such elevated and higher standards of constitutional justice. It has been a frequent judicial refrain that constitutional rights are to be respected not only because they are entrenched in the constitution but also and more importantly because they have a fundamental quality that places them beyond government interference and political meddling. As the American Supreme Court recently opined in 2015 in the same-sex marriage case of *Obergefell*, "The identification and protection of fundamental rights is an enduring part of the judicial duty to interpret the Constitution ... It requires courts to exercise reasoned judgment in identifying interests of the person so fundamental that the State must accord them its respect."[4] This manoeuvre is necessary from the perspective of judicial legitimacy, but is fraught with difficulty from any other angle.

Much the same approach has been taken by the Canadian Supreme Court, albeit in a more typically understated style. With the advent of the Charter in 1982, this fundamentalist posture has become a more common and easier chord to strike. However, Canadian courts have often remarked that such fundamental values and rights pre-existed their explicit crystallization in the Charter's text. Building on the idea that such fundamental rights are in little need of explicit constitutional recognition, judges have been prepared to hold governments to account when such implicit entitlements have been infringed by government.[5] In a ringing endorsement of the fundamentality of constitutional rights, Chief Justice Beverly McLachlin in the *Sauvé* case in 2002 took the high ground and stated unequivocally:

> The core democratic rights of Canadians do not fall within a "range of acceptable alternatives" among which Parliament may pick and choose

at its discretion. Deference may be appropriate on a decision involv-
ing competing social and political policies. It is not appropriate, however, on a decision to limit fundamental rights. This case is not merely a
competition between competing social philosophies. It is for the courts,
unaffected by the shifting winds of public opinion and electoral interests, to safeguard [those rights].[6]

This is a version and defence of constitutionalism that brooks no
equivocation: judges are in the sheltered business of elucidating
enduring truths and must resist the buffeting effects of shifting
public opinion and electoral politics.

These fundamentalist considerations obviously apply in a much
more attenuated way to the Constitution's allocation and distribution of political power within the federalist structure of governance.
There is no philosophical tradition that recommends an enduring
or inalienable schema for such matters; there is very much a political and contested dimension to how this should be designed and
achieved. Nevertheless, there remains a lingering and significant
sense in which it is believed that there is some abstract and neutral
method by which disputes can be resolved. These issues come to
a head in looking to the tension between the authority of the federal government and that of the provinces/states. Although courts
still tend to talk as if there is some innate and harmonious balance
within the Constitution itself, the history of federalism gives the lie
to this half-hearted claim. The courts have struggled to maintain
any consistent or convincing line about how best the division can
and should be made between federal and provincial/state rights.
There persists a sizeable gap between the courts' rhetoric and the
law's reality.

Inside and Outside

It is something of a mug's game to take any document, especially a constitution, at face value. Over the years, constitutional
documents have been pushed and pulled in all directions; these
interpretations have often run in contrary and occasionally

contradictory ways. Indeed, many contend that the best constitutions are those that set trends, but do not fix them and those
that embody general aspirations, but do not spell them out in
detail. Nevertheless, mindful of a whole range of caveats and
conditions, there remains some validity to looking through formal constitutional language to get a rudimentary sense of the
basic values that inform constitutions. There is, of course, a wide
range of rights and responsibilities that are captured, but there
are some core characteristics that are common to the contents of
most modern constitutions. Nevertheless, if constitutional rights
were indeed fundamental, then it would be reasonable and likely
to expect that constitutions would be much the same in terms of
the identity of the rights protected. Although there is considerable overlap among and within different constitutions, there are
also important and telling differences.

After a series of sweeping preambles and aspirational principles (e.g., adherence to the Rule of Law, acknowledgment of
God), almost all constitutions map the existence of different governmental entities and the distribution of power among them.
There is considerable variation in approach and the basic structure
of government is necessarily general in designation and scope.
For example, whereas the United States has a detailed account
of the different organs of government and their relative separate-
ness, Canada has a more impressionistic framework for identifying the location of government power and its valid exercise. Also,
part of these governmental schemes seek to draw the basic out-
lines of the distribution of authority between federal and state/
provincial bodies; there is a basic tension that exists in how this
division should develop and apply as circumstances and conditions change. Disputes over the location, interaction, and limits of
these powers are often less technical than many profess; there are
important and contested matters of politics and policy at the heart
of these disputes.[7] However, it is in the listing and content of constitutional rights that politics come to the fore – these rights can
only be considered as "fundamental" or "neutral" if some foundational decisions have already been made about the ideological
orientation of the constitutional compact.

It is not so much that those rights usually included in the constitutionalized list are somehow inferior or undeserving of serious protection. The rights of freedom of expression, religion and conscience, voting, assembly, and the like are important in any society that aspires to be democratic. However, it is those rights that do not traditionally make the level of constitutionally protected entitlements that raise concerns and tend to expose the skewed and ideological nature of those so-called fundamental rights that are included. At different times and in different places, the range of constitutional rights has been given varied substance and form. The challenge is to be able to differentiate those claims that warrant fundamental status and, therefore, constitutional protection from those rights that are considered to be not unimportant but do not warrant the privileged position of their fundamental counterparts. Without some neutral and principled measure being available to meet this challenge, the prioritizing of constitutional rights will be revealed as a decidedly ideological and partisan act, not a precondition or boundary to the legitimate realm of contested politics. In short, there will be a hierarchy of rights whose probity is based more on ideological predisposition than rational fundamentality.

The basic tension is between those rights that are organized and divided around notions of civil claims and social entitlements. Civil rights are traditionally thought to encompass life, liberty, and security of the person; freedom from cruel and unusual punishment, and arbitrary arrest; fair trial; and freedom of movement, speech, conscience, religion, peaceful assembly, and voting. In contrast, social rights are most often used to include work, social security, leisure, living standards, health, education, and housing. While the former make up the bulk of written constitutions, the latter are conspicuous by their absence in many constitutions. In essence, this divide mirrors the distinguishing characteristics of liberal democrats (who veer towards the civil side) and social democrats (who veer towards the socio-economic side).

Defences of the distinctive treatment of civil and social rights most often hinge on the idea that the civil kind are negative and demand merely forbearance by government, not active provision as the social kind do; the delivery of adequate education and health care is a much more expensive proposition than simply leaving people alone to speak freely or follow their religious impulses. For instance, Bora Laskin, a former Canadian chief justice, argued that civil liberties were more fundamental than social rights and stood on a more "exalted plane" and implicated no particular pattern of economic planning.[8] However, while of only limited force on their face, these arguments reduce fundamentality to a matter of dollars and cents. This seems an unconvincing and not at all reassuring rationale. Presumably, when balance-sheet calculations work out differently, civil rights will be as equally vulnerable to neglect as social rights. Of course, it is not that defenders of civil rights maintain that social rights are unimportant or unworthy of active advancement. Instead, it is that those rights are simply not sufficiently fundamental to deserve the status of constitutional rights. Whereas civil rights should be placed beyond political interference, social rights are open to the ups and downs of contingent political trends.

Although there are more modern constitutions that recognize social rights (even if their enforcement is far from robust or enthusiastic), it should come as no surprise to discover that the liberal democrats have prevailed in Canada and the United States. This general orientation towards a civil libertarian rather than a socioeconomic vision of rights is not all that surprising in an eighteenth-century Constitution (as is the American one), but it is in a document that was entrenched in the last couple of decades of the twentieth century (as was the Canadian one in 1982). While there are provisions that relate to language and public services in the Canadian version that make concessions to a more social and expansive commitment, the overall ambience of the Constitution is distinctly individualist and classically liberal: there are no obvious protections afforded to social entitlements for those least well-off in society.

Again, it needs to be emphasized that these civil rights have been a popular rallying call for the disadvantaged and oppressed in the historical struggle for human dignity and social justice. However, it is hard to see how they are drastically more important than social rights. As John Hart Ely so neatly put it, "Watch most fundamental rights theorists start edging towards the door when someone mentions jobs, food or housing; those are important, sure, but they aren't fundamental."[9] But what is the utility of civil rights if people have no food or shelter? If constitutions are to preserve and promote fundamental rights and values, the failure to guarantee a reasonable standard of living and welfare is a colossal revelation. In blunt terms, the range of rights available demonstrate that constitutional values are very much middle class in their orientation and substance. After all, middle-class people do not worry about where they will sleep each night, what they will do for their next meal, or how they will manage to take care of their children. Moreover, the implicit message is that those rights that are not counted as being fundamental are somehow lesser and can be traded off for other political values without any constitutional comeback.

Accordingly, the notion that some rights are self-evidently or universally agreed to be fundamental is wrong. Any rift around the existence and fundamentality of some rights as opposed to others masks a much deeper and more contestable disagreement that is decidedly and unavoidably ideological in nature. The difference between liberal and social democrats is not a matter of mistaken philosophical premises or technical, let alone economic reckonings. It represents a profound taking of different sides on the operative assumptions of underlying and contrasting political visions. These visions and assumptions are the very stuff of ideological contestation, not an escape from them to some neutral or fundamental realm. As such, the constitutionalists have built their explanatory and prescriptive platform on swampy and political territory, not on solid philosophical ground. Not only are fundamental rights not outside the realm of politics, but they are hostage to it. None of this is to be taken as a demand that socioeconomic rights should be contained in the constitution or that their inclusion would somehow correct the balance and bestow fundamentality on constitutional rights. The simple claim being made is that there are no rights, civil or socio-economic, that exist in a fundamental space that is beyond or above the clash of political ideologies.

A Public Problem

Although there is ample evidence and argument to undercut any claim that the rights presently contained in constitutions are special and fundamental, there are further problems with the constitutionalists' arguments about fundamentality. One particularly thorny problem is with the reach or range of these fundamental rights – against whom can these so-called fundamental rights be called into play and exercised? The fact that such rights are fundamental might be taken to suggest that they are something that can be called upon by citizens to defend themselves against all abuses of power by other citizens and institutions within the polity. As reasonable as that assumption might be, it is wrong. Despite their fundamentality, constitutional rights are considered to be only available in interactions between the government and private individuals. Within the constitutionalist framework, a constitution is concerned primarily with the exercise and effects of public power; it does not assert authority over private power and cannot be invoked by persons in those non-public arenas. It leaves that task to the political and legitimate discretion of those in government. The effect of this bifurcation is not only truly disturbing to those who are genuinely committed to protecting people's actual liberty or equality, but also further undercuts any claim that constitutional rights have a special and fundamental quality.

A revealing entrée into this difficult, but important issue is through an old Canadian case. Fred Christie was a fan of the Montreal Canadiens hockey team and a season-ticket holder at the Montreal Forum. When he tried to order a beer at the Forum's bar in the late 1930s, the bartender refused to serve him: the assistant manager explained that the establishment "extended no courtesy to negroes." Humiliated and angry, Christie brought an action against the Forum. The case went all the way to the Supreme Court of Canada. By a four to one majority, it held that Christie's claim for discrimination failed. For the majority, Justice Thibaudeau Rinfret asserted that "any merchant is free to deal as he may choose with any individual member of the public" and that "it is not a question of motives or reasons for deciding to deal or not to deal; he is free to do either." In his sole dissent, Justice Henry Davis maintained that, whatever the general rule of commerce might be, there was an exception if the government, as in this situation, had given "the licensee ... what is in the nature of a quasi-monopolistic right which involves a corresponding duty to sell to the public."[10] As the Quebec government had not included any legislative power to discriminate, Justice Davis concluded that the bar could not refuse to serve all customers as long as they could pay for a drink.

Many would rightly insist that this decision is a sorry blot on the Canadian legal landscape. Moreover, they might assume that such outrageous and racist behaviour could not possibly be condoned by the courts today over seventy-five years later. However, they would be in for a surprise. As a constitutional matter (regardless of any legislative codes), the Montreal Forum (if it still existed) would still be entitled to refuse to serve patrons like Fred Christie and to do so in a discriminatory manner. The fact is that, although there is now human rights legislation prohibiting and penalizing such conduct, it remains outside the reach of the Constitution and any rights that Fred Christie could claim under it; the Constitution does not extend to private actors, but only applies to government action. While such discriminatory conduct clearly falls foul of the Charter's equality guarantee, that right is only actionable and in play against governmental entities: private actors can be discriminatory with impunity as a constitutional matter. To be blunt, the consequences of such a situation are immense. These consequences of this distinction are of two general kinds.

The first consequence of this distinction between state action and private action is that a hierarchy is created. Despite the claims of constitutionalists about fundamentality, the practical impact is that private power is given greater weight than constitutional rights. For instance, the constitutional right to freedom of expression is understood to allow persons to voice freely their political views. However, they can only do this in particular places. If they own property, they can speak freely and, if they are on public property, they can (within certain reasonable limits) speak freely. But they are not free to enter anyone else's property and speak freely. The property owner has the right to prohibit such interventions. Moreover, the property owner can call upon the state to remove that person from the property. As with Fred Christie's situation, the rights of the property owner trump those of a person who wants to exercise their "fundamental" constitutional rights. Indeed, a strong argument can be made that, by leaving economic wealth outside the purview of constitutional review, modern constitutional law has worked to entrench and exacerbate economic inequality.[11]

Many will consider this situation (i.e., the superiority of the property owner's claim) to be fair and just. Yet it depends upon an acceptance of the idea that, while constitutional rights might be fundamental, they are clearly not as fundamental as the non-constitutional rights of property owners. In other words, whether or not a constitution protects the rights of property owners (and neither the American nor Canadian Constitution does so directly), those rights of property owners are given greater value and protection than those rights extended to all citizens. Furthermore, this means that those with the most property receive, all other things being equal, the most benefits from this situation. For instance, those who own the channels of media communication will be able to spread their political views with relative ease as opposed to those who have no such means or access. While the freedom of the press is, of course, an important value in any society that prides itself on being democratic, it often stands as a cover for the promotion of the particular views of the corporate owners and the accumulation of further profits. Insofar as a democratic society needs a free press, a free society also demands a democratic press.

This leads to the second consequence of the distinction between state action and private action. Not only do property rights receive greater state protection and respect than fundamental constitutional rights, but also some property owners are granted the benefit of those constitutional rights against state action. Although not plain and obvious on the face of constitutional documents, the courts have interpreted the constitution so that corporations and businesses are counted, directly or indirectly, among the holders of constitutional rights. While such enterprises are exempt from constitutional rights being asserted against them, they are able to exercise such rights against government regulation even in their business activities. Canadian tobacco companies have been able to resist advertising restrictions imposed by the federal government as a result of their constitutional rights to free expression. In the United States, a closely held for-profit business was able to avoid government-required health insurance for employees because the coverage of contraceptive devices for women offended its religious views.[12] These decisions place private businesses in an enviable position compared to the general citizenry – they get to claim constitutional rights against government action, but their employees (and others who deal with their business) do not get to rely on their constitutional rights against the businesses.

The upshot of all this is that the constitutionalist vision of constitutional rights is far from fundamental in the sense of being ideologically neutral and above partisan politics. For those attached to such an approach, the main threat to people's autonomy and freedom is considered to be government action, not the intrusions of private power. This stance draws upon a contested and negative vision of liberty that is satisfied when people are left to their own resources to achieve their ambitions; the government's role is to ensure that people's liberty is minimally interfered with by others or itself. Others subscribe to a positive vision of liberty and prefer to represent it as the right to demand from others a greater share of social resources; government might be the only friend that some people have. These visions are not only distinct but also are in competition with each other. The validity of their opposing assertions depends not upon the right to liberty but upon the background conditions and sense of priorities that are seen to support and inform its operation. As such, competing claims about the meaning and extent of constitutional rights can only be resolved by reference to a set of normative values and ideological commitments that are contested and partisan: the constitutionalist pretence that they are somehow fundamental and apolitical is shallow and misleading.

Judicial Interventions

Of course, written constitutions do not interpret themselves: they demand a positive act of meaning-giving in order to bring them to practical life. Under present arrangements, this important and inevitable task falls to the judiciary. As the extension of the various constitutional rights to business and corporations demonstrates, this responsibility offers enormous opportunities to the courts to develop and mould the constitution's fundamental rights in a distinctive manner. As Chief Justice Dickson put it, "the underlying values of a free and democratic society both guarantee the rights in the Charter and, in appropriate circumstances, justify limitations on those rights."[13] Far from being a technical or strictly legal endeavour, this goes to the heart of the historical struggle to confront the most profound issues on the ideological agenda. Moreover, the possibility that the conflict between rights and what might be called the greater public interest can be settled by resort to a prevailing social consensus is illusory and misleading. Such disputes speak to the fractures in community values, not to their availability as a source of normative resolution.

It will come as little surprise, therefore, to learn that the courts have tended to fulfil their interpretive responsibilities by following much the same tack as the constitutional founders and drafters. In short, the judges have read and applied constitutional rights in line with a negative/liberal ideology; they have mostly resisted efforts to follow a more positive/social ideology. A particularly telling example of this is the frustrated struggle to graft certain social rights onto the constitutional text. Both the American and Canadian courts have toyed with the idea of recognizing such social rights, but they have been unwilling to go too far down that road. In regard to welfare entitlements, this adventure not only points up the malleability of constitutional texts but also reveals the general and traditional ideological slant that the courts have taken. It is further evidence that the constitutionalist orientation, at least in its liberal guise, is alive and well.

In the United States, activist efforts were made to protect and develop government social assistance programs by bringing them within the constitutional framework. They met with a measure of success but were stymied by a constitutionalist mindset that prioritized a liberal/negative approach to constitutional rights. In *Goldberg*, the Supreme Court relied upon the due process provisions of the Fourteenth Amendment's equality guarantee: it held that welfare recipients could not have their benefits removed without an evidentiary hearing.[14] However, this was the extent of the Court's solicitude for interests of poor people. In *Dandridge*, it was decided that there was no constitutional obligation to support poor persons: destitute children and families could have their benefits reduced or removed entirely as long as there was no obvious discriminatory treatment or intent.[15] This was a resounding affirmation of the tight hold that a traditional and conservative approach had upon judicial thinking about the nature and bite of constitutional rights.

In Canada, the welfare state has been an established and relatively uncontroversial feature of democratic politics for many decades. Nevertheless, similar efforts have been made to protect and extend the range of social assistance available by bringing them within the ambit of constitutional protection. Despite the frequent judicial assertions that the Charter should be interpreted broadly and that poverty was a major threat to people's dignity, this has not proved to be a fruitful endeavor. In *Gosselin*, the Supreme Court made it plain that the Charter's protection of life, liberty, and security of the person, although it might extend to economic rights, did not place "a positive obligation on the state to ensure that each person enjoys life, liberty or security of the person":[16] persons under age thirty whose welfare benefits were severely reduced had no constitutional claim against the state. Moreover, it also held that the Charter's equality provisions did not apply as the age-restrictions were not discriminatory but ameliorative; they were intended to encourage young people to participate in government work-training schemes. Again, the Court was trapped within a very particular and ideologically oriented way of conceiving of constitutional rights; it was influenced and driven by a view of rights that was largely civil and negative in character, not social and positive. Fundamentality was a cover for more contested political values.

In recent years, this restrictive attitude has been on full display in the context of health care. In the United States and Canada, both Supreme Courts have relied upon a deep and informing ideology in which the state not only has no particular obligation to provide extensive health care but also must not interfere with the rights of individuals to make their own health care arrangements.[17] This has a massively disproportionate effect on poorer people whose only friend or ally in obtaining health care might be government. While richer people are relatively free and able to obtain extensive health care coverage, poorer people are left to their own impoverished devices: health care becomes one more commodity to be sold and secured in the marketplace. To add insult to injury, this is all done in the name of constitutional rights and liberty. Consequently, it can be confidently reported that the "higher" quality of constitutional justice is nothing of the kind; it represents only one – and a very politicized and impoverished one at that – vision of justice.

Conclusion

When it comes to the fundamentality or higher status of constitutional rights, the claims of constitutionalists are difficult to sustain. The constitutional rights included in constitutional enactments are the product of ideological contestation and cannot be understood properly without an acknowledgment of that fact. Consequently, beginning from such a state of affairs, constitutional adjudication is also a practice that cannot avoid the burden and responsibility of political choice. While the originating documents have a built-in partial slant to them, the judges still have sufficient leeway to move within them and, occasionally, against them. As such, courts are not arenas of principle separate from the political realm but are very much a part of that same realm where ideology and political morality conflict. The discourse may be different and the self-understanding of judges may be different, but the work of courts remains embedded in the prevailing context of political engagement and its unavoidable partiality. Unwillingness to see or accept this is not so much an act of forgetting by the constitutionalists as it is a particular kind of willful blindness accompanied by a hollow chorus of angelic laughter; they are so committed to their project that they fail to see or hear the unconvincing preciousness of their stance.

chapter five

Making Changes: Constitutional Updates

Constitutionalists place great stock in the importance of an entrenched constitution. Being the repository of fundamental rights and the settled allocation of governmental powers, there is an understandable tendency to want to protect these arrangements from the partisan fray and ephemeral fixations of day-to-day politics. However, even the most die-hard of constitutionalists concedes that changes might need to be made as later generations come to power and social shifts occur on important moral and political issues. Consequently, most constitutions contain a set of procedures that indicate when and how changes can be made to the constitution. This process is based on the assumption that the constitution should not be capable of amendment in the same and simple manner as ordinary legislation that can be changed or even repealed. After all, according to constitutionalists, constitutions are considered to be of a higher and more fundamental nature than other laws. Therefore, it follows that they should rarely be revisable and only through more exacting procedures. Nevertheless, it is also conceded that those amendment procedures must seek to ensure that, while changes to the constitution cannot be made too easily, constitutional change must not be too difficult, let alone impossible to make.

As even the most well-intentioned constitutionalists admit, this is a very difficult and important challenge to be met. In this chapter, therefore, I will first look at the constitutionalists' focus on stability and the need to prioritize that over other values, especially democracy. Next, I survey the various formal modes of constitutional amendment that are on offer to change the American and Canadian Constitutions. After that, I look at the deeply flawed ways that constitutionalists have sought to circumvent the practical impossibility of formal change by justifying an informal mode of change (i.e., through judicial review). Throughout, I emphasize that a major part of the problem is that no constitution can establish a permanent regime and a democratic regime at the same time. Indeed, the very idea of a definitively just and fully finished constitution that seeks to make democratic instances of popular constitutional change almost unattainable is incompatible with the very idea of a strong democracy. Indeed, it is something of an oxymoron to talk of a perfected constitution in a democratic polity.

Stability and Change

A useful point of departure for exploring constitutional change is through the recent empirical bent in comparative constitutional law. For instance, Zachary Elkins, Tom Ginsberg, and James Melton take the traditional constitutionalist stance to its logical conclusion – a concern with the endurance of national constitutions. At the heart of their project is the question, "Why ... do some constitutions endure, whereas others fail?" Sifting through a data-set that covers every independent state from 1789 to 2005 and that represents 935 constitutions in 200 different nation states, they report that most constitutions only last a couple of decades. This stands in sharp contrast to the longevity of the American Constitution that has endured for over 225 years.[1] The median life-expectancy of national constitutions is nineteen years; this mirrors exactly what Jefferson thought was their "optimal life-span." Destabilizing factors include economic crises, armed conflict, regime change, territorial realignment, and the like. Moreover, these hazards to a constitution's continued existence are not evenly spread; they are vulnerable early on and their likely demise peaks around seventeen years, but this vulnerability decreases until it is lowest around fifty years. For democracies, the average lifespan is about twenty-one years.[2]

While Elkins, Ginsberg, and Melton concede that "there are some real benefits of periodic constitutional replacement," they very much work from the operating assumptions that "a long life is a better life" and that "survival is success." For them, a long life-expectancy is the best indicator of constitutional health; the longer constitutions live, the better a nation's constitutional health can be considered to be. Of course, there will be exceptions to this, but these only manage to prove the statistical rule. So wedded to these assumptions are Elkins, Ginsberg, and Melton that they conclude their impressive study with the telling summation that "the life expectancy of constitutions, if anything, decreased over the last 200 years ... [such that], unlike human beings, the health of constitutions is not getting better with modernity."[3]

This alleged connection between life expectancy and constitutional health is as misleading as it is revealing. The fact that the American Constitution has endured for more than two centuries is insufficient on its own to warrant high praise or a clean bill of health. The course and content of American history need to be assessed against some independent and evaluative criteria. The implicit standard behind this view is that of institutional order and political stability; the celebration of "endurance" places these values ahead of all others – states with old constitutions are in general better than those which change constitutions more frequently.

The problem, as ever, is that such an assessment is indifferent to the need for and appeal of democracy as a guiding political value. Within this constitutionalist framework, democracy is considered to be one of the distinctly secondary attributes that might be thought of as instrumental to the continuing life and endurance of constitutions. Elkins, Ginsberg, and Melton's work recommends that democratic stability (as opposed to non-democratic governance) is found to be closely tied to constitutional stability and that "enduring constitutions are good for young democracies."[4] They go on to crystalize and defend an explicitly constitutionalist approach to national governance. As they maintain:

Constitutions generate a set of inviolable principles and more specific provisions to which future law and government activity more general must conform. This function ... is vital to the functioning of democracy. Without a commitment to a higher law, the state operates for the short-term benefit of those in power or the current majority ... By limiting the scope of government and recommitting politicians to respect certain limits, constitutions make government possible.[5]

Consequently, it is not that constitutionalists are hostile to democracy, but rather that they do not take its demands or dynamics very seriously; theirs is a cautious and inhibited approach. They concede that democracy is necessary and praiseworthy, but they view it as far from being an animating or central feature of modern constitutional arrangements. This is particularly so in regard to change and amendment.

This constitutionalist antipathy towards popular participation is evidenced by the prevailing approaches to constitutional reform. The motivating idea is that change should be infrequent because the stability of a legal order is a primary value to be protected. However, most constitutionalists do concede that a large part of the constitution's democratic legitimacy rests on the fact that it can be changed through popular and participatory means. Consequently, by way of compromise, liberal constitutions tend to make the process of amendment so arduous that few proposals for change are able to meet its stringent requirements. These limits on constitutional reform extend well beyond basic liberties to the entire structure of government institutions. The amendment provisions of most modern constitutions underwrite the permanence of the constitutional order. Indeed, these provisions typically involve a set of requirements that are more difficult to meet than those followed when the constitution was originally adopted. While most constitutions are adopted by some form of majority rule, constitutional amendments are traditionally associated with super-majorities and other obstacles designed to decrease the possibility of important transformations. Some constitutions even place some clauses outside the scope of the general amendment procedure. Taken together, these considerations highlight the fear of constitutional change that characterizes constitutionalism.[6]

Of particular significance in this discussion is the fact that the typical liberal constitution rarely includes mechanisms that increase popular participation during times of important constitutional transformation or crisis. For example, there is little reference to the popular election of delegates that deliberate in extraordinary assemblies and whose proposals have to be ratified in referendums: democratic legitimacy is thought to be satisfied by the involvement and authority of ordinary representatives and their executive leaders. Instead, there is a deep commitment to the idea that constitutions must be insulated from the reach of regular change through vigorous and participatory democratic processes. As such, by containing and confining democratic participation, the constitution is given political priority over democracy: the rough-and-tumble character of democratic politics is considered too risky, too untamed, and too disruptive for the angelic world of the constitutionalist. The history of constitutional change in North America is entirely reflective of these constitutionalist fears and inhibitions.

A Formal Affair

The written constitutions of the United States and Canada are reasonably representative of the kind of formal provisions that are relied upon to facilitate (or stymie) changes in a polity's constitutional structure and commitments. On their face, these formal procedures are particularly demanding; they require a broad and concerted political will to change existing arrangements. However, in practice, their requirements have proven to be even more difficult to meet; they have worked to place a tight chokehold on constitutional change. Indeed, in line with a constitutionalist mindset, they seem designed to ensure, whether by design or default, that formal changes to the constitutional structure are of a rare and exceptional kind. This, of course, has led to more informal avenues being explored.

Under the American Constitution, the amendment process is contained in Article V. While it was created by a successful revolution, it makes future changes in the Constitution extremely difficult to effect: it is one of the most demanding constitutional amendment processes in the world.[7] Under Article V, two-thirds of both houses of Congress may propose amendments or two-thirds of the state legislatures may apply for a constitutional convention for proposing amendments. These proposals must then be ratified by three-fourths of state legislatures or by three-fourths of special state conventions; there is no requirement for the President's involvement. As history demonstrates, this has been a difficult standard to meet. From a strong democratic viewpoint, Article V not only makes constitutional amendments almost impossible to adopt, it also makes their unlikely adoption a very non-participatory event; an amendment to the Constitution is left in the exclusive and representative hands of government officials, albeit elected ones.

With such formidable hurdles, it is not surprising that the American Constitution has been amended only twenty-seven times in over two centuries. Over 11,500 amendments have been proposed in Congress, but only thirty-three have been passed by Congress and only twenty-seven ratified by the necessary number of states. The first ten amendments were passed in 1791 and comprised the Bill of Rights; these were supplemented in the mid-nineteenth century after the Civil War and added rights to due process, equality, voting, and the like. The 26th Amendment in 1971 extended the right to vote to those eighteen years of age and older, and the 27th Amendment in 1992 concerned "congressional compensation." Indeed, it is telling that the ratification of the 27th Amendment took 200 years to be completed; it was ratified in 1992 after being originally presented by James Madison in 1789. All told, therefore, Article V seems to be as much an amendment-prevention process as an amendment rule: it entrenches a constitutional compact from over 200 years ago and is even antithetical to the ambitions of its original enactors.

The story in Canada is not much better. Prior to 1982, constitutional amendments were simply a matter of legislative amendments by the British Parliament. In almost 120 years, there were slightly over twenty amendments made. Most of these were of a structural nature that recognized more directly the growing independence of Canada as being no longer a colonial state. However, with the patriation of the Constitution in 1982,[8] a formal amendment process was entrenched. This is limited to government-approved changes and imposes some very severe limitations on when changes can be made. In general, the amending formula requires that there must be resolutions passed by the federal Parliament and at least two-thirds of the provincial legislative bodies with at least 50 per cent of the national population. This effectively means that change cannot occur without the involvement of either the two largest provinces, Ontario and Quebec (although, as was the case with the original patriation of the Constitution, it can be done with both being approved). However, some parts of the Constitution can only be amended through the unanimous consent of the federal Parliament and the legislative bodies of all provinces; these include the office of the Queen and Governor General, the composition of the Supreme Court, the use of the French or English language, and the amendment procedure itself. This offers a very high bulwark to be climbed; it places an effective block on any future amendment that is intended to be substantial and structural.

Further, in Canada, minor amendments can be made if they affect only one province and if that province's legislature and the federal Parliament agree. Since 1982, there have been several minor amendments of this type that affect only one province, such as the nature of provincial schooling in Newfoundland or in Quebec. However, there have been two major efforts to effect significant constitutional change, but they have been unsuccessful; unanimity has proved to be elusive. In 1987, the so-called Meech Lake Accord sought to deal with Quebec's antagonism to the original 1982 patriated Constitution (to which it had refused to participate in its formation or to give its willing assent); it failed to be ratified by all the required ten provinces. A second attempt was made in 1992 through the so-called Charlottetown Accord, but it was defeated in a national referendum. Many politicians and constitutional scholars now concede that any substantial and formal changes to Canada's Constitution are highly unlikely. As in the United States, such constitutional amendments have become a close-to-impossible enterprise. A final nail in the coffin of constitutional change was the very recent decision of the Canadian Supreme Court that prevented the federal government's self-initiated and independent efforts to change the composition and format of the federal second chamber, the Senate.[9] Consequently, the formal constitutions of the United States and Canada seem to be destined to endure as they are for many decades to come, regardless of any democratic appetite or drive for change. This leaves the task of changing the constitutions to other, even less democratic bodies – the courts have become the major medium through which change has occurred.

In both Canada and the United States, there are other available, but presently unused processes for amending the Constitutions. Article V of the American Constitution does envisage an alternative route for constitutional changes. It stipulates that two-thirds of the state legislatures (presently thirty-four) can "call a convention for proposing amendments." While there have been several serious calls for such a convention to be held, this method of amendment has never been used. However, in the case of the first ten amendments and the 17th Amendment, as the number of states needed for the calling of such a convention was approached, Congress moved to introduce the desired amendments. This is a profound example of the antipathy towards direct and active democratic participation. The unwillingness to rely on a more democratic procedure speaks volumes about the established political elites' fear and distrust of such a potentially unruly and wide-ranging process. In line with a constitutionalist mentality, it prioritizes stability and elite control over popular and regular participation in constitutional matters.

In Canada, there is no such convention-calling option: all constitutional power remains within the firm control of government officials and representatives. However, there is an aspect of the written constitution that does countenance the incorporation of a more directly democratic method for change. This is the so-called override provision. Under s. 33 of the Constitution Act 1982, the federal Parliament or provincial legislature alone may expressly declare that an act "shall operate notwithstanding a provision included in s. 2 or ss. 7–15" of the Charter of Rights. In effect, this covers all the basic rights except those connected with voting. To effect such an override, a simple majority is all that needs be attained in the federal Parliament or legislative assembly; the override can only apply to those matters within the overriding government's jurisdiction.

While this is a powerful tool, it has been used infrequently: only Saskatchewan, Quebec, and one territory have utilized it, although its use has been threatened by other provinces. It has never been initiated by the federal government. Indeed, although the inclusion of this provision was an essential component of the initial deal to achieve patriation of the Constitution,[10] its existence has been treated as aberrational and somehow offensive to Canada's constitutional and democratic tradition. This is evidence of the tenacious hold that a constitutionalist approach has on the democratic process – the exercise of popular authority, albeit through elected representatives, is considered to be almost illegitimate and, at best, a very last resort option. To make matters worse, change through judicial interpretation and intervention has now become not only the default process but the apparently preferred approach.

So understood, the American stance against constitutional conventions and the Canadian demonization of the override provision confirm that democracy does not register high on the constitutionalist scale of political values; constitutionalists clearly prefer courts over conventions as a conduit for democratic action. Under the tutelage of a constitutionalist mindset, both constitutions seem to be constructed and represented as being an almost fixed and unchanging framework for political debate and action. But, at least as far as the legal and political elite are concerned, there is a convenient acceptance that the avenues for informal change will work smoothly and will produce results that, if not always in line with elite values, will not be entirely antagonistic to them over the long run. Although there might well be occasions on which the courts make changes that do reflect and/or advance popular interests, these relatively small and occasional concessions work to legitimize the larger constitutionalist status quo. In contrast, it can be stated that the more democratic such amendment procedures become in thrust and origin, the more legitimate those changes to the Constitution would become.

Plus C'est la Même Chose, Plus Ça Change

Of course, the upshot of having an almost next-to-impossible-to-use amendment process is not that no changes in constitutional arrangements happen. It is difficult to identify or imagine any society whose constitution, even if its form remains the same, also stays fixed in substance and meaning over any extended period of time. This is especially the case in common law jurisdictions, like the United States and Canada. The contrary situation applies – change occurs by other and even less democratic means than those amendment opportunities provided by the written constitution itself. The major and celebrated means is, of course, judicial interpretation. While jurists and politicians may pay lip service to the fundamental quality of the nation's founding and formal written documents, they know that this is only the beginning of the process for establishing (and re-establishing) constitutional meaning. Amendment is simply one kind of change that is more formal and less technical. It is the more informal action in the judicial forums of the constitutional order where most of the constitutional action occurs. Indeed, these informal changes are often, although not always, more significant than formal amendments to the written constitutional text. While there is no simple or fixed causal relation in play, the informal amendment process through judicial intervention is inextricably linked to the formal amendment process in "that an informal amendment process exists because formal amendment is so difficult."[11]

Changes, even of a large and significant nature, occur through the courts although the formal process of constitutional change itself remains unused and unchanged. In both the United States and Canada, changes in constitutional law have happened at a steady and continuous pace. While taking place under the guise of interpretation and under claims that such alterations are incremental and marginal, there have been some monumental changes in the regime of constitutional structures and rights. If *Brown* (de-segregated schooling) and *Roe* (abortion) in the United States and *Halpern* (same-sex marriage) and *Carter* (doctor-assisted suicide) in Canada, for example,[12] are treated as merely interpretive adjustments, then the supposed distinction between interpretation and amendment becomes so blurred and so unreliable as to be nebulous. Constitutional history shows that there is no change that is so big that it could not be achieved informally (and even in spite of the written constitution) if the political forces are sufficiently aligned to demand or facilitate it. It is only when there is insufficient support for change (particularly from the elites) that the formal amendment process will appear as a brute obstacle to change.[13] Otherwise, change will proceed with little concern for the distinction between legal interpretation and constitutional amendment and between the formal and informal practices of change.

In implementing and defending this adventurous practice, the courts have used a range of doctrinal devices in constitutional law and adjudication. History is replete with examples of where the courts have been impressively creative in fulfilling their interpretive task. Each manoeuvre has the effect of relegating the formal constitution to a secondary and occasionally dispensable source of judicial constraint. Some of these include:

- Things that are in the written parts of the constitution can move in and out of the constitution over time.
- Things that are not in written parts of the constitution can move in and out of the constitution over time.
- Things that are written in the constitution can be limited and controlled by things that are not written in the constitution.
- Things that are written in the constitution can take on different and occasionally contradictory meanings over time.
- Things that are written in the constitution can be circumvented by things that are not written in the constitution.[14]

Trying to make sense out of what the judges of the Supreme Court are doing on these occasions has been an enduring preoccupation of lawyers and jurists. Within the jurisprudential canon, there exists a whole range of theories that claim to offer an account of what it is that judges do and should do in fulfilling their institutional role of interpreting and applying the Constitution in a society that claims to be democratic in organization and ambition.[15] At the heart of these legitimating efforts are the imperatives of formal objectivity and substantive justice. There is a felt need to provide some method or technique by which judges can give meaning to the Constitution. Moreover, this must be both capable of giving substantive direction and consistency to decisions reached and that itself is not reducible to only their own (or the jurist's) political and moral commitments. While many, like Ronald Dworkin or Antonio Scalia, have taken the high road of defending larger theories of constitutional justice, others, like Cass Sunstein and Richard Fallon, have opted for the low road and taken a more self-consciously modest approach. In this, they each have followed in the established tradition of Herbert Wechsler by proposing that justices perform their difficult task in a way that is distinguishable from "the *ad hoc* in politics" by its reliance upon principled reasons that "in their generality and their neutrality transcend any immediate result that is involved."[16] The persistent claim is that legal interpretation and judicial decision-making can and should be performed in a way that distinguishes it from the more open-ended ideological debates that are the stuff of outright political struggle.

Of course, no self-respecting modern lawyer or legal theorist pretends that law is Holmes's "brooding omnipresence in the sky" that lends itself to formulaic application or provides robotic predictability.[17] It is trite learning that legitimacy cannot be grounded in law as a sealed system of normative directives. Nevertheless, there still remains a tenacious commitment and aspiration to the idea that there is truly a difference between what the law is and what judges say that it is: law may be given a different accent by a different judge, but it is all part of law's own and distinctive language. While the constitutionalists' exhortations to "stick to the law" are seductive, they offer little suggestion of how such a seemingly prosaic practice can be achieved in constitutional law. At a theoretical level, three initial observations come to mind. First, the ascertainment of legal principles is itself fraught with political contamination and content. "Established" is simply a way of saying that certain moral or political commitments, once controversial, are now accepted by the legal community as settled; this is less an endorsement of the principles' apolitical nature and more an acknowledgment that general acceptance is a form of political validation. Second, the range of established principles is extremely broad and often encompasses competing maxims; there is no neutral or non-political way to select between contradictory principles. Third, even if it is possible to isolate a relevant and exclusive legal principle, it is far from obvious how that general principle can be applied to particular facts in an entirely objective or impartial manner. In short, there is no purely technical and non-political way to engage in a principled mode of adjudication. While this is true for almost all law, it is especially pertinent to constitutional law.

Two recent chief justices have offered their own response to this challenge. Former Canadian chief justice Beverley McLachlin offered a spirited defence against "fashionable" attacks on the democratic legitimacy of judicial power. Contending that it is wrong to characterize the judiciary as excessively powerful or political, she insisted that, at every turn, the potentially despotic power of judges is hedged and controlled by the traditions, conventions, and rules of the law itself: "judges are guided by precedents which dictate particular results, quite apart from the judge's personal views" and "the power of the courts is constrained by many factors, including their own rules, which forbid the exercise of power beyond their own statutory and constitutional mandate."[18] The problem with this is that her defence begs the very question to be answered. She assumes the operative force of the supposed restraints – legal precedents, constitutional conventions, and judicial traditions – whose very existence and efficacy is at stake and in contention. Indeed, McLachlin makes the case against herself. She demonstrates that Supreme Court justices judge others by an allegedly independently created and independently existing set of standards that are as much part of the argumentative discourse as their application of them.

American Chief Justice John Roberts offers an even less convincing effort to legitimize the courts' activities. He contends that "judges are like [baseball] umpires – umpires don't make the rules; they apply them." He sealed this modest portrayal of judicial virtue by insisting that "judges have to have the humility to recognize that they operate within a system of precedent, shaped by other judges equally striving to live up to the judicial oath."[19] While this humble depiction of judicial responsibility – "it's my job to call balls and strikes and not to pitch or bat" – will strike a reassuring chord with some, it fails to recognize the history and nature of the judicial role generally. Judges are much more than umpires. Indeed, the whole analogy between judging and umpiring is misleading and inaccurate. As far as their judicial duties go, history demonstrates that judges are players and very much part of the political action. It is less about *whether* they change the rules than about *how* they do so. Staying with the baseball analogy, while some umpires claim to call balls and strikes "as they see 'em," others assert that "they ain't nothin' 'til I call 'em." People might be fated to play a baseball of the judges' choosing, but the judges are also very much part of the game; they play by the rules as well as change the rules as they go along. In legal terms, what counts as not only "balls" and "strikes" but also what counts as "baseball" changes over time. And it is the judges, for better and worse, who are the purveyors and guardians of many of these changes.

Accordingly, in a society that claims to be devoted to the ideas and practices of democratic legitimacy, it is far from clear why the courts are considered to be the preferred, more suitable, and more appropriate institution to speak and act on the people's behalf. To put it more pointedly, if the courts are assumed to have democratic legitimacy, then democratic legitimacy is a very thin device and counts for little in the general political scheme of things. Despite the protestations of constitutionalists, the courts are neither oper-ated nor constituted in line with popular will or representative viewpoints. As John Hart Ely put it, "we may grant until we're blue in the face that legislatures aren't wholly democratic but that isn't going to make courts more democratic than legislatures."[20] Indeed, the democratic legitimacy of the courts is somewhat perversely grounded in their willingness to act as a check on and even barrier to popular and direct expressions of constituent power. This seems to put democracy firmly under the control of the constitution. At best, democracy is reduced to merely one value in a much broader range of constitutional commitments.[21] In blunt terms, the vaunted Rule of Law is considered to be little more than the spruced-up

Rule of Judges. As such, the informal amendment of the constitution raises challenges that go to the heart of the democratic compact – how do judges rein in abuses of power without themselves engaging in similar abuses of power?

An Empirical Turn

There is an ample literature that seeks to describe and document the claim that constitutional law is politics. While more traditional accounts accept that fundamental values are at stake in constitutional adjudication, the general approach is "confession and avoidance" – constitutional law is political, but in a principled and, therefore, defensible way.[22] There has also been a more radical account that insists that courts are inevitably and inescapably political in that judges cannot fulfil their constitutional duties without making contested and ideological choices; the history of constitutional law is a record of the various twists and turns that judges, individually and collectively, make in bending both the constitutional text and legal doctrine to a particular political and often shifting political outlook.[23] However, in recent years, there has been another intervention into the constitutional debate over whether courts and judges perform in a strictly legal or clearly ideological way in meeting the demands of a constitutionalist approach. Rather than rely on the tools of political theory and philosophical analysis, the considerable resources of social science have been brought to bear on the jurisprudential challenge presented by constitutionalism.

Relying on a range of statistical and empirical methods, both quantitative (e.g., factor analysis, bivariate correlation and logistic regression) and qualitative (e.g., personal interviews and published reflections), the established consensus is that it is simply not possible to make a credible claim that judges' personal ideologies do not influence and affect their approach to the policy matters that come before them. While judges may not be dogmatic or even consistent in their value-choices over subject matter and over time, they do follow a general political line in doing their work. Not surprisingly, American judges tend to be more entrenched and less nuanced in this regard than their Canadian counterparts.[24] This is not to say that "legal analysis" plays no role in the work, but that it is not the sole or dominant factor in their decision-making. Moreover, it must be remembered that, once that understanding is accepted, even the following of established rules can no longer be viewed as an entirely apolitical process.

In more recent Canadian work, there has been a certain refinement of these basic claims. It is claimed that courts' decisions are influenced not only by judges' personal ideologies about substantive values but also by their institutional and strategic considerations about the courts' role in broader governance matters, especially the legitimacy of the relationship between courts and legislatures and the changing flow of public opinion. This, of course, does not so much defeat the argument that "justices' backgrounds, personal values, and ideological predilections play a significant role in decision-making."[25] Instead, it offers a more subtle appreciation of what counts as "ideological." Rather than think of it exclusively in substantive terms, it broadens and deepens the analysis to include institutional and strategic concerns. Such an insight is to be welcomed, and it reinforces rather than undercuts the basic idea that "law is politics" in the sense that constitutional law is not primarily about any determinative kind of internal doctrinal or interpretive dynamic. When appreciated in this more sophisticated way, the basic insight of this empirical turn confirms that "judges' decisions are a function of what they prefer to do, tempered by what they think they ought to do, but constrained by what they perceive is feasible to do."[26] This is a convincing explanation of law-is-politics.

As important and revealing as the results of this scholarly turn is, it is very limited in its general ambitions and prescriptive value. It offers telling insights into how the courts work and confounds many of the claims by judges and mainstream jurists about the democratic legitimacy of that activity. However, from a constitutionalist (or anti-constitutionalist) standpoint, it has little to contribute. Any critical inquiry into the work of the courts in constitutional law must confront not only what judges do but also what they can do and should do. At best, these empirical-oriented commentators are agnostic about whether the judges can or should fulfil their judicial duties as demanded and outlined by most constitutional theorists; they stick to describing and explaining what judges do, whether or not they might or should be able to do something else. In contrast, I take the view that what judges do is the only thing that they can do (i.e., act politically). The question of whether they should do something different is simply not relevant or pressing. In other words, whatever judges decide to do or claim that they do, they will not be able to do anything other than act politically. Accordingly, judges and jurists must not waste valuable time and energy in developing more abstract and inventive proposals of how to act in a way that fulfils their constitutionalist mandate, but rethink the whole basis of that constitutionalist approach.

Finally, there is one argument, more implicit than express, in the work of these empirical scholars that might be considered pertinent to the constitution/democracy debate. It is that, once it is accepted that an important factor or limitation on the judges' personal preferences is that they are mindful of and often in step with popular opinion, then it can be asserted that the courts are not undemocratic because they do respond to and "reflect changing popular will."[27] This is an intriguing notion, but it is unconvincing. It seems that the impact of popular opinion is not direct, but is filtered through the judges' own political leanings. Moreover, it assumes that there is such a thing as a uniform and almost monolithic "popular will" that could be followed: the most difficult decisions for courts are those (e.g., same-sex marriage and euthanasia) in which there is no social consensus and there is a very polarized set of views in play. The division of judgments within Supreme Courts attests to this idea. Moreover, constitutional decisions tend to be as much the shapers of public opinion as they are the effects of it. Indeed, a troubling effect of this explanatory dynamic is that there has been a "judicialization of politics" that works to undermine further the foundational constitutionalist claim that there is and can be a clear and maintainable separation between law and politics.[28] In short, law and politics are so interrelated that any effort to treat them as independent spheres is doomed to fail.

Conclusion

Despite their roseate rhetoric, it can be reported that the constitutionalists have not done at all well in meeting this central challenge of explaining constitutional change as they need to. They have hewed much too closely to the need for constitutional stability and stymied democratic changes. They seem to maintain that constitutions can be perfected and, once this ideal state of affairs is achieved, there is no need for substantial change. In contrast, I have insisted that there is no such thing as a "perfect constitution." The very idea that such an ideally finalized constitution can be designed and implemented is not only so much pie-in-the-sky thinking but also is anathema to the democrat. Too often, constitutions place checks and limits on democratic participation in the name of some other set of vaunted truths or elite-favouring values. For the strong democrat, it is formal constitutions and their institutional paraphernalia that do more to inhibit and dull democracy's emancipatory potential than to nurture and fulfil it. The process of constitutional change speaks forcefully and critically to that dynamic – constitutionalism trumps and weakens democracy.

chapter six

Striving for Democracy:
An Endless Journey?

A constant refrain for the constitutionalist chorus is that the nature of judicial review in constitutional law is explainable in terms of the courts' relationship with the legislature. The basic idea is that courts have such strong and demanding expectations placed upon them to be apolitical and neutral because legislatures are freely entitled to act in openly ideological and partisan ways; legislatures are democratically elected, but courts are not. As such, as representatives of the citizenry, legislators have an obvious democratic legitimacy that eludes judges and is unavailable to their work. This places enormous and, as I have sought to demonstrate, unsustainable pressure on courts to achieve some *modus operandi* that somehow underwrites their suspect democratic and counter-majoritarian status. However, in the same way that I have "laughed" at those who try to defend the apolitical and neutral work of the courts on constitutional law and chastised them for their "forgetfulness," I now want to shift tack and direct that same critical attitude towards the work of legislatures. Despite claims that legislatures are necessarily democratic in their origins and, therefore, legitimate in their authority, I will argue that the democratic legitimacy of legislatures is much hyped and much overrated. A strong account of democracy places much greater expectations on legislators than presently exists.

The corollary of the defence of courts as democratic partners or institutional checks is that legislatures are represented as being almost devoid of principled dynamics and as acting in an entirely partisan fashion. This ought not to be the case. Democracy demands that politicians can (and do so more often than many claim) and should be required to aspire to a much more rigorous practice of political engagement. Accordingly, in this chapter, I will revisit the whole idea of democracy and recommend what a strong and uncompromising commitment to democracy would entail. The second part explores how such a democratic commitment works as both a substantive politics and as a procedural process; there is much more to democracy than simply allowing popular participation through voting. I then examine the state of democracy in contemporary United States and Canada; it is a far from encouraging snapshot. Finally, I take seriously the need to subject legislatures to a root-and-branch reform that will oblige them to live up to democratic expectations. Throughout the chapter, the main gist will be that, although legislatures can be and are captured by elite interests and regularly perform well below their democratic best, they come out ahead of courts in terms of their democratic potential and improvability. As such, courts are fatally flawed in ways that legislatures are not when it comes to democracy.

Revisiting Democracy

"Democracy" is one of the most relied upon and one of the most contested terms in the political and legal lexicon. Indeed, its malleable and expansive nature is a large part of its enduring appeal. At its heart, the democratic ideal is about the idea that people should rule over themselves and that government should be by the people, for the people, and of the people. This is a demanding ambition and practice that operates as much as an aspiration as a practical road map. Accordingly, societies are not so much democratic or undemocratic, but more or less democratic in their relative merits. In an important manner of speaking, the smaller that the gap is between the rulers and the ruled and between the powerful and the powerless, the more democratic that society will be. At bottom, democracy is thoroughly and deeply anti-elite. As such, any society or polity that claims to be democratic will be disposed to take measures to facilitate "closing the gap" between its governing elites and its governed majority.

In "closing the gap," any sensible democratic theory must pay attention to both the "formal" and "substantive" elements of democracy. While it will be essential to ensure that there exist appropriate venues and processes through which people can participate in government and hold it accountable, it will also be equally important to look at the substantive conditions in which people live so that their participation can be relatively equal and robust. As such, electoral participation is not a full or true measure of a society's democratic health. At its starkest, it would be difficult to suggest that a country which extended the vote to all citizens was deserving of democratic accolades if the largest part of the population lived in miserable conditions, with a short life expectancy, and with little education or employment prospects. This would be more a travesty of the democratic ideal than its realization.

Democracy is better thought of as a social way of life in which everything that affects the conditions of people's lives is potentially encompassed; democracy is a value and process which can inform all aspects of social life. Viewed this way, democracy is the commitment *par excellence* to the idea that almost all choices and actions have political roots and political consequences: people can tackle those politics within a framework within which their active participation is more important than (or, at least, as important as) that of elected representatives and appointed elites of political sages. In particular, democracy need not be construed as simply a set of processes and practices tagged on to a particular political ideology, whether it be liberalism, conservatism, socialism, or whatever. Indeed, democracy is a mode of life, an *ethos*, a way of day-to-day living within which the best of such ideologies and political commitments can be harnessed and their excesses jettisoned. In that sense, the robust brogue of democratic politics insists that the liberal, libertarian, or socialist is only one kind of democrat and that the democrat is not only one kind of liberal, libertarian, or socialist.

Accordingly, this strong approach to democracy is very strategic and political; it is not merely conceptual or philosophical. Rather than talk in absolute terms about the overall democratic

quality of society, it is preferable to concentrate on those measures which will make a society more democratic. From this
standpoint, "democracy" is not a black-and-white idea or practice. A society is not democratic or undemocratic: it is a matter of
shading and degree depending on a contextual and contingent
assessment. Any intervention or initiative that moves society
from a less democratic state of affairs to a more democratic one
is to be encouraged. While it will be necessary to make trade-offs
within a democratic society (i.e., as between distribution and pro-
duction, freedom and equality), it is unnecessary and ill-advised
to make trade-offs *with* democracy. To think in such terms is to
misunderstand democracy.

As such, the type of democratic commitment that I propose and
defend is pragmatic and strategic rather than idealistic or absolut-
ist. The primary consideration in any effort to effect change will
always be – *what present measures will best increase the greater participation and control which people have over those institutions and practices
which most affect their lives today?*[1] While it is better that more are
involved more of the time than less are involved less of the time,
it seems counterproductive to deny a reform proposal or strategy
the term "democratic" because it does not involve everyone all
the time. In the democratic playbook, the best ought not to be the
enemy of the good. As such, this democratic spectrum operates
with a dimmer switch, not an off switch; it is calibrated along a
relative and interactive grid of participation.

That being the case, it is possible to highlight several strategic
and pragmatic commitments against which any particular proposal or reform to advance the democratic project can be assessed.
These are what I will call "the five basic precepts of democratic
advancement." Taken together and mindful of their shaded application, they confirm the emancipatory and transformative potential that lies within democracy:

- *More extensive participation is better than less extensive* – Because
  democracy is as concerned with the pedigree of power as
  the effects of power, any state of affairs which multiplies and
  broadens the number of locations, whether public or private,

in which participation is possible is more likely to advance democracy than not;

- *More participation is better than less participation* – Because involvement is a benefit in itself and can beget a taste for even further involvement, any state of affairs which increases the degree of direct as well as indirect or substantive as well as formal participation is more likely to advance democracy than not;
- *More equal participation is better than less equal participation* – Because people can experience genuine participation only if their involvement is effective and counts for something, any state of affairs which tends to ensure that no one has more power than anyone else and that citizens can engage on an equal footing is more likely to advance democracy than not;
- *More responsibility is better than less responsibility* – Because people cannot be expected to be involved all the time in all locations in all circumstances on all issues, any state of affairs which renders those with temporary power more accountable to others who do not is more likely to advance democracy than not; and
- *More transparency is better than less transparency* – Because people must be educated and informed if their participation is to be meaningful and telling, any state of affairs which increases the amount of knowledge to which people have access and the capacity to weigh it is more likely to advance democracy than not.

A Democratic Gamble

Democracy does not have all the answers to life's challenges. Indeed, a strongly democratic approach to governance embraces the idea that there are no once-and-for-all right answers. It eschews the notion that there is one way to govern and one way to live. Instead, it nurtures a lived practice that seeks to accommodate difference of opinion rather than do away with it. As such, a democratic society is never "the finished product." There is always more to be done. By contemplating a regime of popular self-government which not only allows for, but relies upon participation by citizens in the formulation and enactment of laws that govern their lives, it has no truck with the idea that there is some independent or ahistorical basis on which to measure and approve different policies and laws. This does not mean that politics will lose any reflective or self-critical edge; it will not be a steady stream of majoritarian prejudice writ large. The idea and practice of democracy extends power to present generations on the condition that it does not inhibit or constrain the similar entitlement of later generations. This is a gamble, but it is one that is worth taking. The implications of this for constitutions in democratic societies are obvious.

In its strong incarnation, therefore, democracy stakes out its turf by demonstrating faith in the responsibility and capacity of political participants, widely assembled and deeply acknowledged, to do "the right thing." This does not mean that there will be no checks and balances on the popular imagination or its passing preferences. However, any checks and balances that are in place will be dictated by the need to maximize participation, not to corral it. To date, democracy has too often been viewed as more the icing on the political cake than part of the cake itself. Indeed, the constant pressure to constrain and cabin democracy in the service of some other overarching ambition is plain evidence of a fearful acknowledgment of democracy's potential to subvert the status quo. In many ways, the appeal of a more republican account of democratic governance, while defended on pragmatic grounds, is understandable. But it works too easily to distance ordinary people both collectively and individually from the levers and institutions of genuine power. Indeed, this turn in democratic theory has a tendency to legitimate a slightly spruced-up version of the status quo and to negate the potential of people to be the governors as well as the governed.[2]

By ensuring that democracy's broad mandate (i.e., including social and economic as well as political matters) and deep mandate (i.e., requiring regular sustained acts of participation at local, regional and national levels) are both respected, it will better ensure that the citizenry become full participants in the political process. To do this demands that there are greater efforts to pluralize and circulate the sites and situations in which democracy is at work. By being flexible and pragmatic, democrats can accept that compromise as well as conviction are important quali-ties. In developing a truly democratic mode of political participa-tion and involvement, a further gamble is made that, as citizens self-govern through participatory processes of deliberation and decision-making, they will themselves evolve into more engaged and generous citizens.[3] This is because, within a practical under-standing of participatory democracy, citizenship requires more than voting from the individual members of society; it requires that individuals actively engage in creating and implementing the legal rules and political processes that shape their own and their communities' lives. This concept of democratic participation necessarily entails direct deliberation, direct action and direct contribution.

For this depth and extent of participation to occur, there must be dialogue that demands more than allowing people to air their views; it demands a realistic opportunity to have such participa-tion respected and responded to by others. While not all citizens are prepared to participate in every decision-making process, what is important is that individuals understand that they can participate if they so choose. Whetting their appetite to partici-pate, they must be provided with both the requisite opportuni-ties to do so as well as the support necessary to do so. As such, a strong and participatory democracy needs a mix of representa-tive and direct processes that can reinforce and complement each other. There ought to be no kind of debate or decision that is out-side the scope or ken of popular participation. To countenance such a possibility is to slide back into a debilitating form of elit-ism that characterizes what presently passes for democratic prac-tice. Despite the efforts of elites – whether educational, social, economic, cultural, ethnic, religious, or legal – to engage in the self-preserving exercise of persuading ordinary people that they cannot be trusted to do "the right thing," ordinary citizens are as up to the task of fulfilling their democratic responsibilities as any elite cadre of officials.

Much is made of the claim that, no matter how noble or com-mendable the democratic ambition, society is now too large and too complex to believe that ordinary citizens can be entrusted with the full responsibilities of governing themselves. This is a common refrain of established elites. It is true, of course, that citizens do not necessarily possess all the expertise that is required to engage in sustained debate and make informed decisions. However, this does not mean that so-called experts should dominate and push to the sides those with less knowledge and experience. When it comes to government and governance matters, experts should be put in service to the citizenry and not usurp the citizenry's prerogative to be the final decision-makers. This will take humility on the part of experts, but it will be a necessary part of the democratic compact. This is no more apparent than in the case of courts and judges: it is important that the legal tail does not wag the democratic dog.

Sadly, the roots of such an undemocratic tendency to place great weight and authority on the opinions of experts runs deep. The origins of both the American and Canadian system of governance and constitutionalism are highly elitist in thrust and direction. The structure and identities of both countries were not only forged in elitist circumstances but also were engineered to keep a check on the increasing emancipation of ordinary people. The late eighteenth-century Founding Fathers of the American Constitution were a privileged elite who were determined to ensure that any role for the public in affairs of state was limited and occasional: "the public voice, pronounced by the representatives of the people, will be more consonant to the public good than if pronounced by the people themselves."[4] But what is more troubling is that this attitude has persisted and democracy has become an increasingly weak and insipid version of its best self. In 1985, Canadian Prime Minister Brain Mulroney asserted that the advent of an entrenched Constitution and Charter of Rights a few years earlier ensured that Canadians "live in the kind of democracy for which we are all grateful."[5] However, although the constitutionalist roots of both countries might be thoroughly aristocratic and oligarchic, this does not mean that the resulting governmental schemes are beyond revision and transformation in line with a genuine democratic and anti-elitist sensibility.

Where We Are At

Few people would maintain that democracy as the central mode of political organization was in the best of health. While there has been a marked increase in the number of countries that can claim to be "democratic," the on-the-ground operation of those democratic processes is far from reassuring. At end of the Second World War, there were only twelve nations with a political system that could plausibly be termed "democratic." Today, over seventy years later, there are around 115 out of about 195 countries that can be counted as being brought under the general rubric of democracy. This is an encouraging development. However, beneath this optimistic and general appearance, there is a more pessimistic and troubling set of indicia. For instance, although the franchise is broad in principle, there remains problems with the registration of voters and their capacity to vote. Consequently, it is important to delve into the murkier specifics to get a more rounded sense of the actual state of democracy in the modern world, especially in the United States and Canada.[6]

The general trend is that voting has been in decline over the past decades. It is rarely more than 75 per cent of registered voters (except in those few countries where voting is mandatory) and is more generally less than 60 per cent. Also, the percentage of the overall population that is voting has also been in decline. As a result, when this fact is combined with a first-past-the-post system, victory goes to the party, candidate, or president that has not only much less than 50 per cent of those votes cast but also an even lower percentage when measured against the overall population. For example, President Donald Trump was elected with less votes than his Democratic opponent, Hillary Clinton, due to the system of the electoral colleges. Also, he was elected with less than 26.3 per cent of the eligible voting population. The situation is not dissimilar in Canada where the government of Justin Trudeau secured a substantial majority of seats in Parliament with about 39.5 per cent of the vote cast. As the total vote was only about 68.3 per cent of the general voting population, Trudeau's Liberal Party won with less than 30 per cent of the total voting population.

6.1 United States Voting-Eligible Population (VEP) turnout rates, 1789–2016

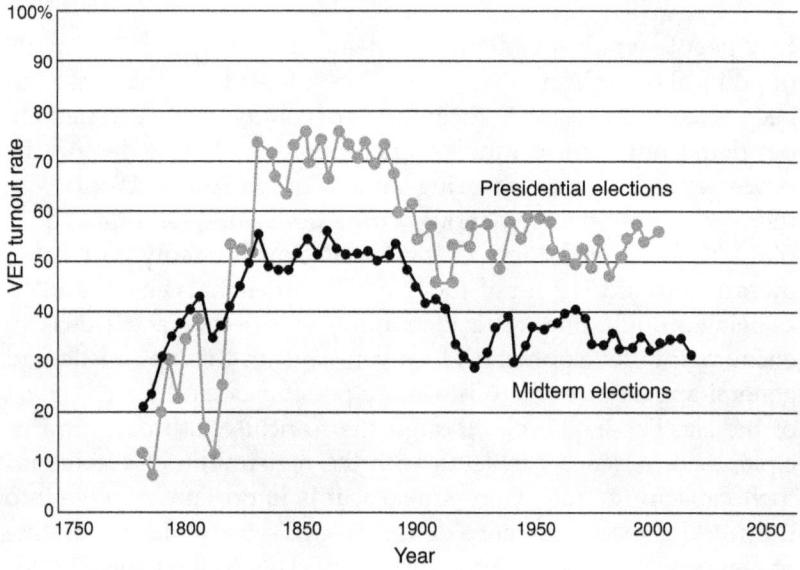

6.2 Voter turnout, 1867–present

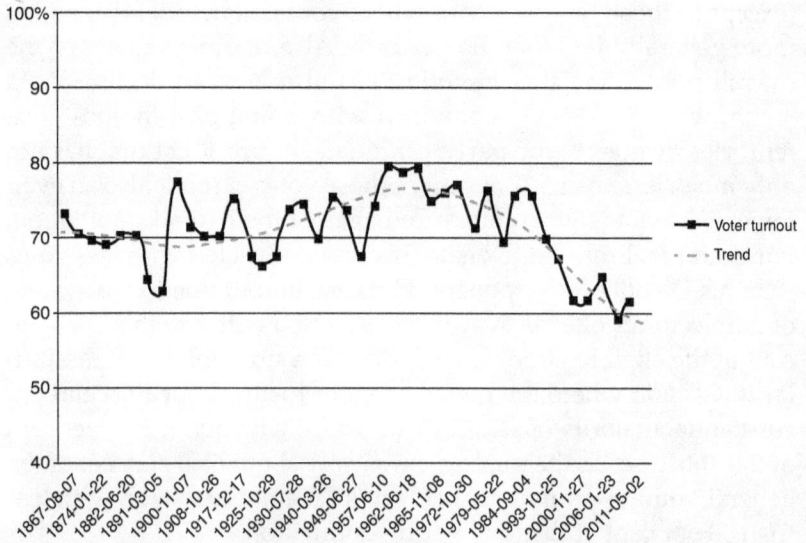

Of course, general voting patterns reveal only a small and distorting portion of the overall picture. Digging deeper, the integrity and efficacy of the democratic process becomes even more fragile and suspect. This is a matter of considerable concern when all the things that are done, large and small, by government in the name of democratic legitimacy are remembered:

- Young adults vote at much lower rates (around 30 per cent in the United States and 57 per cent in Canada) than older adults (around 65 per cent in the United States and 78 per cent in Canada);
- More women (around 64 per cent and 80 per cent) vote than men (around 59 per cent and 78 per cent);
- More white persons (around 65 per cent and 77 per cent) vote than persons of colour (around 52 per cent and 71 per cent); and
- More higher-educated persons (around 71 per cent and 86 per cent) vote than lower-educated persons (around 30 per cent and 66 per cent).

In the most general terms, this represents a sorry story. In recent years in the United States and Canada, elections have become something of a joke as a basis for political participation and governmental legitimacy. They have devolved into something of a circus-like spectacle that, aided and abetted by the general press as well as social media, are as much about popular entertainment as political emancipation; apathy is the induced state of the electorate who have become indifferent and often alienated from the political process. This has played into the hands of existing and established elites. Indeed, as Tocqueville warned over 175 years ago, democracy has fulfilled its tendency, if left unguarded and taken for granted, to degenerate into a "soft despotism."[7] Although there is a formal appearance of democratic vigour, the lived reality belies such a prognosis. It is not so much that citizens participate in self-government, but that they have occasional and limited opportunities to select those members of the elite that will govern them. Being able to cast one vote in a national election of millions of voters for an executive leader (who is granted enormous powers during their tenure in both the United States and Canada) from a constricted list of elite candidates is hardly the stuff of democratic participation. It is not surprising that almost more people fail to vote than those who vote for the successful candidate.

The most recent Canadian federal election in 2019 points up some of the deep problems with the present system of first-past-the-post democratic elections. Apart from the fact that such elections only occur every four years and are meant to be the main source of popular participation, the overall participation rate was about 66 per cent of citizens eligible to vote (who account for about 85 per cent of resident Canadians over eighteen). Although the Liberals won slightly less of the popular vote at 33 per cent to the Conservatives 34 per cent, they received the most seats (157) and were able to form a minority government; the Conservatives only obtained 121 seats. This means that the new Liberal government received only about 22 per cent of the overall eligible voting population. The Liberals' support was concentrated in central Ontario and Eastern Canada; there was no Liberal representation in Alberta or Saskatchewan. Also, although the New Democratic Party received 16 per cent of the popular vote, it only won twenty-four (7 per cent) of the available 338 parliamentary seats. Even more starkly, the Green Party won 7 per cent of the popular vote, but obtained only three seats (less than 1 per cent), whereas the Bloc Québécois won almost the same percentage of the popular vote (8 per cent), but obtained thirty-two seats (almost 10 per cent). These kinds of outcomes are hardly reassuring from a democratic standpoint. Indeed, they are downright depressing – the results in a first-past-the-post process are so definitive, yet so flawed.

All in all, therefore, democracy is in a far from healthy state. The rhetoric of democratic legitimacy is a long stretch away from the reality. Apart from the token act of occasional voting, people have very little role in the formulation and enactment of the laws and policies that govern them. As a result, they become the passive recipients of government initiatives, not active participants in their creation. This puts into serious question the validity of political systems in which the "masses are relegated to voting for representatives, joining interest groups (few of which have adopted internal participatory procedures), and providing the elites with new recruits."[8] As such, elections offer a patina of legitimacy and little

of genuine substance to societies that claim to fly under the ennobling banner of democracy, but are ruled by elites. The best that
this can deliver is a faux democracy that offers "benign elitism" on
behalf of the people rather than a government by and of the people.

Legislators and Judges

While there has been a sharp increase in the twentieth century in
those countries that might be termed "democratic" (although the
depth and extent of that commitment, of course, is controversial),
there has also been another countervailing increase that puts that
more general democratic turn into serious question. During the
shift to democracy and perhaps as part of that shift, there has been
a hefty increase in the number of written constitutions adopted.
Since 1787, a form of constitutional review has steadily gained
popularity; 83 per cent of the world's constitutions include it
today.[9] This has brought with it a marked extension of the reliance
on courts to determine the constitutionality of legislative and executive action and, therefore, their limits and legitimacy. Such a set of
occurrences is nothing new in North America. Judicial review has
long been a feature of both the Canadian and American schemes
of governance. However, this more modern and global trend has
tended to underline the fact that, as the involvement of ordinary
people in government has increased, so has the development of
alternative mechanisms and institutions to curb and marginalize
that impact.

The main governmental institution that is not elected (and to
that extent accountable to the people) is the courts. To the democrat, it is ironic at best that the agency tasked with interpreting
and applying the constitution is the least democratic one. However, constitutionalists see this as the courts' great virtue. Far from
being a threat to or usurpation of democracy, courts are viewed
as a necessary supplement and component of a truly functioning
democracy. Constitutionalists go to great and elaborate lengths
to persuade anyone who will listen that judges work to temper
and restrain the excesses of majoritarian politics because they are

insulated from the democratic pressures of partisan politics and accountability. However, this places a weight upon the court that is too heavy for them to carry – they must reason and decide cases in ways that are distinctly legal and objective as opposed to political and partisan. But, from a democratic standpoint, the courts are asked to perform an impossible task and, not surprisingly, buckle under the weight of institutional expectation. Rather than serve as the custodians of the democratic project, the courts house a coterie of elite officials who represent a severe obstacle to the fulfilment of a strong democracy's constitutional project.

By describing their primary challenge and *raison d'être* as being to check the tyrannical excesses of the majority, judges set themselves up to be one more elite who think that they know what is best for people. In this sense, there has been little change since the advent of judicial review. The constitutional founders at least had the good grace to admit to such a stance. As Canada's minister of justice announced to Parliament during the constitutional debate in 1981, the Charter will do "a great service to Canada by taking [controversial] problems away from political debate and allowing the matter to be debated, argued, coolly before the courts with precedent and so on."[10] However, this stance merely exacerbates the problem. A truly participatory mode of democratic government demands citizens wrest control of decision-making from such faux democrats as judges. The best that a judicial body, like the Supreme Court, can do is to function as a benevolent dictator. And this is the antithesis of democracy. Although judges might well act in good faith and strive to render decisions that are consonant with the ideals and commitments of democracy, they are at bottom one more elite (and an especially powerful one at that) that views the democratic mandate through the lens of their own dispositions and values.[11]

A favoured constitutionalist defence of courts is that they are "forums of principle." Whereas legislatures are portrayed as sites of outright ideological contestation, the courts are offered as a safe haven in which principled and detached reasoning might prevail. But this is a false depiction of both legislatures and courts. First, there is nothing special or privileged about principled reasoning. Much depends on what the particular principle is; there is little that is meritorious about espousing and defending principles (e.g., racist or sexist precepts) that will do more harm than good. Also, commitment to some grand principle, even if tolerable in thrust and direction, is not guaranteed to lead to just, let alone democratic, outcomes. Finally, principles are simply another way of dressing partisan or ideological values in more respectable or facially neutral garb. The whole premise, therefore, that principled reasoning is capable of being contrasted and distinguished from partisan posturing is unconvincing; it is a mode of intellectual elitism to think otherwise.

As long as the false perception is maintained that legislatures are heated sites of raw ideological head-banging and courts are cooler enclaves of principled reflection, this will authorize judges to impose a whole slate of contested values as constitutional truths. In particular, it will allow them to impose procedural and substantive constraints on governments that will hinder their ability to regulate markets, redistribute wealth, design health care systems, protect the environment, and organize the electoral process. And this is exactly what the courts have done in the guise of making and developing constitutional law.[12] Although defended by the constitutionalists as rational and objective decisions about higher values and neutral commitments that protect or advance democracy, the courts have managed to establish a loose but decidedly ideological set of restraints on the freedom of legislative assemblies and democratically elected officials.

None of this is intended to suggest or recommend that legislatures and their members are presently acting in some ideal or desirable way from a democratic perspective. If judges are not as principled as constitutionalists insist, then legislators are not as crudely ideological as the same constitutionalists complain. However, the solution for dealing with the shortcomings of legislative debate and action is most decidedly not giving power to an entirely unelected body to act as a countervailing and supposedly principled makeweight. The problems of legislatures should be dealt with by ensuring that the ambitions of democracy are more fully and consistently met by legislators. The deficiencies of legislators must be dealt with by and within democracy, not by

resort to non-democratic means or forums. Indeed, if all government actors, including judges and legislators, are failing to live up
to the standards expected within a democracy, it is more democracy that is required, not less democracy. Accordingly, judges and
legislators are neither principled nor ideological by virtue of their
status as legislators or judges. There is nothing about democracy
that allows or condones the type of debased standards that seem
to be reflected by present political debate. A genuine commitment
to strong democracy implies and demands that political debate be
both intense and respectful.

The whole depiction of courts as principled correctives and
checks on legislative activities depends on an understanding of
legislatures' work as being unprincipled and crassly ideological
in make-up and performance. This is mistaken. The responsibility
of legislators is or ought to be about carrying through on the need
to represent all citizens; there is no pressure under existing theories for legislatures to rise above the lowest standards and expectations so that politics can fulfil a more noble (and democratic) image
of itself. Consequently, under the constitutionalists' dichotomy
between ideological legislators and principled judges, legislators
are left free and clear to disregard the substantive values and aspirations of democratic governance. Indeed, the existence of courts
as constitutional arbiters relieves legislatures of their responsibility to confront their own democratic failings and foibles: "an
additional layer of final review by courts adds little to the process
except a rather insulting form of disenfranchisement and a legalistic obfuscation of the moral issues at stake in our disagreements
about rights."[13]

A different and more thoroughly democratic account has the
virtue of pressing legislators to take more seriously the duty to
address the justness of their actions against a broader and more
substantive account of democracy. If and when this occurs, the role
and superiority of the courts become a much less seductive idea.
Although there might well be a continuing need to take a second
look at legislative policies and enactments, this no longer has to fall
to an elite and unelected institution.[14] As long as critics remain hostage to a constitutionalist approach to democracy and believe that

the answer to democracy's problems is less, not more democracy, then popular politics will remain stifled and hijacked by elite institutions and interests. Moreover, if the democratic compatibility of judges and legislators is to be compared, then this must be done by evaluating them when they are both at their best. When this is done, there can be little doubt that legislators will come out ahead. This is not simply because they will get it right (as if this was a viable or realistic possibility anyway). It is because legislators will not be checking or correcting democracy's impulses and initiatives, but because they will be acting in the name of democracy and with its validating support. In short, while judges work against the democratic process, legislators work with and in favour of it.

In contrast to the constitutionalist, therefore, the strong democrat maintains that, if provided with better and more extensive institutional opportunities to participate in their own governance, people will cultivate a greater appetite and aptitude for political engagement. The critical gamble is that, if elitism breeds largely subordinates, then democracy might well beget mainly democrats. In short, what is needed is more democracy, not less. Indeed, democracy will only be possible if there is a willingness to move beyond its presently anemic and weak form and to engineer changes that bring it closer to its more full-blooded potential. Unfortunately, traditional constitutionalist thought exhibits only a weak commitment to democracy as part of a stronger commitment to constitutionalism more generally and judicial review more particularly.

Conclusion

To revamp the legislative and executive process in line with greater popular participation and political accountability will require a monumental effort. Any changes – proportional representation, recall legislation, accountability audits, genuine ministerial responsibility, referenda, and so on – must themselves be products of the very democratic process that is to be enhanced. There are no easy solutions to the current undemocratic trends. However, any improvement to the democratic status in Canada or the United

States will not come from increased interventions by judges in the micro-management of governmental policies. Indeed, judicial review does more harm than good. If there is a democratic desire to reign in judges, there must also be a commitment to ensuring that elected politicians and officials are living up to their own and demanding constitutional and democratic responsibilities. At present, they are palpably not. But simply construing the democratic challenge as being one about whether judges stay out of or stray onto the political terrain is to misrepresent the problem and, therefore, to hamper any genuine solutions. There needs to be a whole rethinking about the very existence of courts and judges as we presently know them.

chapter seven

An Elite Concern:
Inequality and Democracy

Alexis de Tocqueville was more prescient than many give him credit for. In his two-volume masterpiece, *Democracy in America*, he charted the role and dynamics of democracy in the United States of America during the mid-nineteenth century. Although far from being an outright champion of democracy, he saw that the old aristocratic order had to give way to an emerging and more populist mode of governance. However, as much as he chronicled what he thought to be the apparent dangers of democracy (i.e., excessive equality, mass rule), he was also attuned to what he saw as the future threats to democracy. Tocqueville was worried that democracy might be allowed to slide into a "soft despotism": power would still remain with a select few, but they would be less narrow than the old aristocratic order but more beholden to an educated and bureaucratic elite.[1] In particular, he saw that the Industrial Revolution might generate its own subversive menace through the creation of a plutocratic class; authority would reside with those who could amass property, control the market, and influence governmental policy. In making these predictions, Tocqueville was not far off the historical mark; he was prescient and pertinent about today's major challenges to democracy.

The relationship between wealth and democracy (or, more accurately, between money and democracy and its distorting effect on governance) is a perennial problem. Indeed, like the increasing disparities in income and wealth throughout North America, the dependence of democracy on money is getting worse, not better.

This deeply troubling dynamic affects both legislative and judicial realms of government. Accordingly, in this chapter, I will look at the overall problem of elite influence and control of democratic institutions and processes. The second section explores how modern elites tend to be defined by money; this turns government into a plutocracy more than anything else. In the third section, I examine the populist pushback against elitism and seek to make sense of the very different kinds of populism in play; some are troublingly anti-democratic in spirit and substance, but others hold more democratic potential. Finally, I look at the effect that all this has on the judicial role and its performance: society's increasing economic inequality casts a significant shadow over the workings of constitutionalism and the development of constitutional law.

Democracy and Elitism

Nothing has come easy to the democrat. The history of democracy is a tale of resistance and courage. And it is no different today. Democracy is under pressure everywhere. It is not only struggling to win new national recruits around the world, but it is having grave difficulty in those nations where it is already considered to be established and enabling. This is particularly true of those Old World states that are intent on promoting its benefits to more sceptical New World countries: domestic threats to democratic practices and ideals threaten to undermine the whole appeal and exemplar of democratic government. Moreover, this seeming crisis is mirrored by the state of democratic theorizing. Commentators and scholars lock horns over what is and is not demanded by a genuine commitment to democratic governance. In particular, the fundamental tensions between security and freedom, stability and change, and representative and popular participation have become more evident and acute. From all sides of the political spectrum, there is considered to be a crisis of confidence in the capacity of democracy alone to meet the challenges of the modern age. Indeed, there seems to be a deep anxiety that, while democracy has a role to play in contemporary governance, there are definite limits to its provenance and authority.[2] In short, debate rages over the extent to which democracy has to be confined and circumscribed in the name of some larger and more encompassing political ideal.

Democracy, of course, is one of the most uttered, yet least specified ideas in the political lexicon. It can and has been utilized by many different people in many different situations to defend or promote many different states of affairs. Against such a definitional backdrop, it is not surprising that democracy's ideals have often been belied and occasionally betrayed by their practical realization. In Greece during the sixth century BC, there was less a democracy and more a timocracy in which wealth and land ownership (not to mention being male and unenslaved) were a condition of the voting franchise. Indeed, a sceptical review of democracy's history suggests that there is almost a disturbing inverse correlation between the extension of the franchise and a reduction in the amount of power in which the enfranchised can participate: the more that people are allowed to participate as an electorate, the less that is left to their decision-making authority. Despite the constant invocation of "democracy" as a rallying cry and source of legitimation for governmental decisions, there has been a distinct distrust of ordinary citizens' capacity to participate fully, freely, frequently and actively in their own governance.

In the twentieth century, democracy came to be associated almost exclusively with the institutional and competitive struggle for people's votes by those leaders who sought political power: popular participation was reduced to little more than the demand for free and fair elections among multiple political parties in a context of relatively open information. Along with the judicially enforced protection of basic civil rights, this constrained idea of democracy as "elective aristocracy" has come to dominate and is now the accepted gold standard of democratic legitimacy for almost all contemporary regimes; the goal of a more extensive popular participation seems to have fallen by the wayside. Yet this radical separation between the rulers and ruled is a very far cry from what democracy meant just a few centuries ago, even to its opponents.[3] By and large, democrats have been thwarted in their efforts to institutionalize the belief that the governed are not only competent to elect their governors but also entitled to make political judgments for themselves about all issue, not only some of the substantive ones.

Suffice it to say that the core of the democratic ideal is the preference for ordering power and authority in line with the views and requirements of the citizenry. The *cri de coeur* of democrats has been the need to involve people as fully as possible in all those institutions and agencies which influence and affect their daily lives. "Weak" and "strong" forms of democracy can be distinguished by the extent of the gap between rulers and ruled and between powerful and powerless: the smaller the gap, the more strongly democratic that society will be. Indeed, a strong form of democracy recommends that there is no dichotomy of governing elite and governed majority; there will be an almost flat structure of government such that the "state" will be more disaggregated and indistinct. Instead, people will play as full and as frequent a role as possible in the governance of their society. Whereas weak democracy contents itself with claiming that it is a government *for* the people, strong democracy aims to approximate as closely as practicable to governance *for* and *by* the people. At its strongest, democracy is seen to be not only a formal device for tallying people's preferences but also an extensive process for popular participation in governance and a substantive vision of politics.

Viewed this way, democracy is opposed to all efforts to accumulate and exercise power by the few over the many. Indeed, history shows that the main contemporary challenge for democracy remains less whether the majority will ride roughshod over the minority, but whether a minority – be it a moneyed few, a judicial aristocracy, a political elite, a bureaucratic oligarchy, a workers group, an academic cabal or a corporate organization – will ride roughshod over the majority. The democratic initiative recommends against all such divisions; it seeks to exert a centrifugal rather than a centripetal influence on power. As such, power is not the problem in itself, but its aggregation in unaccountable cliques and privileged circles is. Too often, democracy and its institutions are hijacked by some elite, even if claiming to speak and act for the interests of all society. No matter how well intentioned or benign, the claims by elite factions to know better than an informed citizenry ought always to be resisted. Understood as a social as well as a political way of life, democracy aims to empower people so that they can tackle all matters that affect their lives within an organizational framework in which their active participation and control are its most important and distinguishing features.

An Economic Kind of Elite

Democracy's admonition against elite control has been its ever-present and central theme. While the nature of that elite and its dominating strategies have changed throughout history, there has been a constant and consistent effort by the rich (capitalist or aristocratic) to laud it over the poor (serfs, workers, and consumers). Although this has occasionally been done for benign and ostensibly egalitarian purposes, the resounding fact is that, unlike love (and perhaps even then), power and influence can be bought. The basic idea is that, in every system, democratic or otherwise, the rich tend to have more political power. From this, it tends to follow that the greater inequality in the distribution of wealth, the greater the disparity between rich and poor in terms of political power. In such a political state of affairs, there will be less of a democracy in any true sense of the word and more of a plutocracy. However, this drive for power and influence can be done directly through and under cover of the democratic process: "democracy's assassins use the very institutions of democracy ... to kill it."[4] Indeed, there can be no more perverse politics than utilizing the processes and institutions of a democratic polity to undermine and disable that very same democracy.

In these early decades of the twenty-first century, plutocrats are no longer content to stand in the wings and pull the strings of political leaders and governments; they more brazenly assume up-front positions of political and democratic leadership for themselves. The effect of this elitist state of affairs is to sideline democracy or, even worse, to reduce it to a gaudy charade in which the wealthy piper really does call the tune. Form triumphs over substance by converting it into its own empty reflection: the glib message become the political medium. Public discourse becomes hostage to economics and people think of themselves primarily as consumers rather than citizens. In such a set of circumstances, it is hardly surprising that the elite-busting potential of democracy has been stymied and co-opted. Consequently, businesses are able to advance their own agenda and interests by shaping government policy, and are also able to sideline or negate the impact of average citizens. None of this is new or novel. The inimitable Aristotle remains pertinent in his judgment – "the real difference between democracy and oligarchy is poverty and wealth: the rich are few and the poor are many ... where the poor rule, that is democracy."[5] As such, it is important to understand the current extent of wealth disparity in North America today. It is almost the case that as goes inequality, so goes democracy.

It follows, therefore, that elections are not the only or the most revealing measure of a country's democratic health. When the overall substantive and relative conditions of people's lives are taken into account, this also presents grounds for more concern; there is little that is encouraging. It might be less troubling for there to be a maldistribution of substantive resources and opportunities if the most recent trends were towards reducing or modifying it. However, over the past decade or so, the trend has been in the opposite direction – the extent of inequality in wealth and income is getting worse and the gap between the haves and the have-nots is increasing. The relatively stable inequality of the post-war years has been replaced by a troubling decades-long trend of increasing concentration of income and wealth at the top. In 2015, even in Canada, the richest 20 per cent of held more than twelve times the share of total incomes than the share of the poorest 20 per cent. The middle class was "disappearing" and the incomes of the poorest remained abysmal.[6] This is an appalling state of affairs by any standard, let alone a democratic one.

In the United States, although the average standard of living has increased in recent decades, relative inequality has also accelerated to alarming degrees:

- The top 10 per cent have increased their share of overall wealth from 68 per cent to 73 per cent, and the bottom 10 per cent have had their share of wealth decrease from 6 per cent to 4 per cent over the past twenty years;
- The average income of the richest 10 per cent is about seven times more than that of the poorest 10 per cent – this is significantly higher than it was twenty years ago;
- Women earn about 80 per cent of what men earn – this ratio improved over the past twenty years or so, but has lately plateaued;
- Child poverty rates are around 22 per cent and 14 per cent – this is higher than in other rich nations; and
- All these measures are significantly worse for persons of colour than for white persons.[7]

Although there is a general perception that Canada has less inequality than the United States, the Canadian figures are very similar to the American ones. Moreover, in Canada, there is no inheritance tax as there is in the United States. These stark snapshots are revealing:

7.1 Household wealth distribution, percentage share of wealth (or net worth)

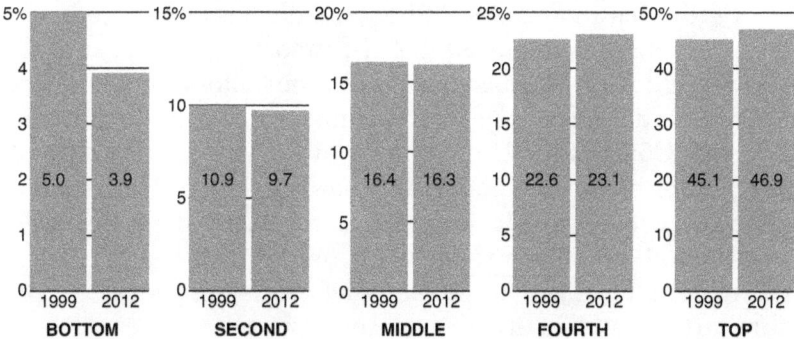

7.2 Holdings of family wealth, trillions of 2013 US dollars

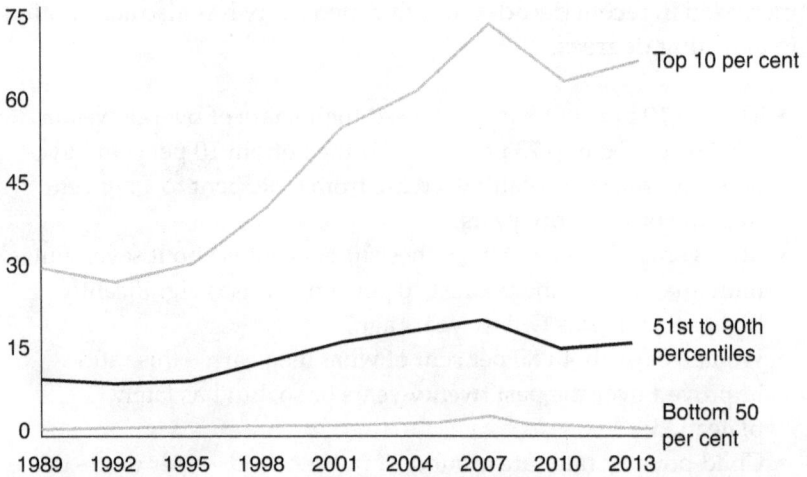

It is surely the case that this kind of significant and increasing socio-economic inequality is not conducive to democratic health. The idea that different people with vastly different resources might be able to participate and affect equally the course of political debate and government decision-making is entirely untenable. In a world in which "money talks," the wealthy can exert influence over not only those in power but also the general election process itself. The amount of money that is spent during elections is enormous and has a distinct tendency to skew attitudes and results. Although there has been a creditable series of attempts to curtail the disproportionate impact of the wealthy elite on elections throughout the history of democracy, recent decades have seen a very significant U-turn. In 2010, the Supreme Court of the United States in *Citizens United* declared, as a matter of constitutional law, that legislative efforts to regulate large corporate contributions to electoral parties were impermissible.[8] This is somewhat ironic in that constitutionalists have felt obliged to defend such decisions as being both non-partisan and justified by democracy itself.

While there is no need or warrant for absolute equality (as this would stifle individual initiative and require constant governmental supervision and readjustment), a commitment to democracy suggests that everyone, not only some and certainly not only a few, should share not only in the governance of society but also in the good and bad fortune of that society. To be genuine democratic participants, people must be emancipated from bondage of all kinds – economic, social, and cultural: franchise and finance have become mutually dependent and increasingly so in recent years. The extent of participation by lowly citizens in those power-centres that affect their lives is the measure of democratic progress. Equality of opportunity demands more than the dismantling of formal barriers to participation, it also requires continuing substantive and affirmative measures to actualize those opportunities and possibilities. Consequently, democracy's commitment to social and political life must be as substantive as it is procedural. This presents a challenge that goes to the very nub of the democratic imperative. Vladimir Lenin's blunt summary of the state of democratic politics remains as accurate today as it was a century ago: "The oppressed are allowed once every few years to decide which particular representatives of the oppressing class shall represent and repress them in Parliament."[9]

A Populist Pushback?

It should come as no surprise that there has been a backlash to this growing and debilitating elitism. Although it is only now manifesting itself fully, it has been a long time coming. Across the world, an anti-elite populism seems to have taken hold. This push-back against the elite nature of government and its policies has not only fired up many people's imaginations and actions but it has also resulted in real effects upon the direction of government policy and the approach of its elected representatives. A popular resentment has been given voice and acquired votes in the process. These self-styled populists, like Donald Trump in the United States and Doug Ford in Ontario, Canada, took advantage of the elitist capture of democracy and capitalized on the disenchantment and alienation of large sectors of the citizenry. Moreover, this trend is far from being over; it can reasonably be argued that this is the beginning, not the middle or the end, of a new phase in politics and governance. Populism appears to address a simmering resentment by opening up the closed spaces of political power to more popular and previously side-lined interests.

The causes and cures of this situation are, of course, complicated and contested. Some maintain that populism is not a problem, but a solution; it is a corrective, not a threat to democracy's excesses. The difficulty with this debate is that it views the populist pushback as having only one core character and one core alternative account of politics and its possibilities. This is mistaken. Like most political movements and ideologies, populism has very different dimensions and can move in different directions. Most populist initiatives are motivated by an anti-elitist dynamic and, to that degree, share a similar opposition to the existing state of liberal democratic politics; they agree that it is really a faux liberalism with democracy tagged on for affect. However, beyond that, they have a very different diagnoses of that elitism's ills and the remedial action to be taken. As such, populism can be divided into two very different camps.[10] On the one side, there is a right-wing populism (that is presently in the ascendancy); it is both illiberal and non-democratic. On the other side, there is a left-wing populism that has a strong and alternative history; it seeks to hitch liberalism to a more democratic and egalitarian commitment. In short, the right-wing version threatens democracy, whereas the left-wing kind is more a corrective in the name of enhanced democracy.

The common motifs and characteristics of right-wing populism are tribalistic, exclusionary, and authoritarian. Even in its less overtly racist mode, it resorts to the need to give voice and influence to "the people" as a cover for the expression of a closed and insular identity: it posits a homogenous body of loyal citizens who have been excluded from governance by a corrupt elite and who share one general identity, a common sense of morality, and a unified political will. Elitism itself, economic or otherwise, is not the problem, but its present sullied composition and unpopular practices as adjudged by the populists' own sectarian lights are. As such, right-wing populists are more than willing to put their political faith in a leader who can distil and give expression to the essence of the people and their resentment and marginalization. These populists do not oppose any form of democracy *per se*, but, like liberals, view it as having only limited and instrumental use. But whereas liberals at least have a concern for minorities, populists maintain that majority rule is what counts because minorities have no legitimate claim to full representation unless they acknowledge the "true" and collective values of the people. This strain of populism is a close sibling to fascism and its public excesses.

In contrast, left-wing populism has very different roots and ideals; it stands almost entirely against the prescriptions and tendencies of right-wing populism. It offers a challenge to elitism that is more sustained and uncompromising, but it is distinctly not in the name of a divisive and sectarian politics. Eschewing any cult of leadership, it does not seek to replace one elite with another and even more narrow one. Whereas right-wing populism is tribalistic, exclusionary, and authoritarian, its left-wing kind is emancipatory, pluralistic, and non-hegemonic. Drawing on the experiences and grievances of farmers and workers, it strives to recognize the people as being a diverse and pluralistic group that share a common exclusion but are not bound by any forced or debilitating conformity. In regard to democracy, it recognizes and accepts that both liberalism and right-wing populism use it only in so far as it advances and is compatible with other values and attainments. As such, a left-wing populism does not abandon all the gains and potentialities (in terms of advancing individual freedoms) but seeks to place them within a more secure and egalitarian context; it embraces the animating idea that a degree of economic equality is necessary for there to be real freedom and political equality.

In this regard, left-wing populism resonates with Franklin Roosevelt's proposal for an Economic Bill of Rights – "necessitous men are not free men."[11] Under the aegis of liberal democracy, the neutral state only treats people equally in their abstraction; there is almost no acceptance of the radically unequal socio-economic circumstances shaping people's lives. This abstracting strategy might work in polities where there is some semblance of economic equality. But it will not work in societies, like modern-day Canada and the United States, where there is an enormous disparity of wealth and economic resources. The provision of liberal rights as framed will not ameliorate let alone fundamentally change this state of affairs in which some have enormous surpluses and others struggle for the basic necessities. At best, liberal citizens are middle-class and white men who are comfortable in their economic well-being and largely content in their future social prospects for themselves and their families. Unfortunately, the continuation and complicity of liberal naivety, at best, will simply perpetuate existing economic divisions and make matters worse.

It should be clear from my analysis to date that I reject right-wing populism out-of-hand and stand firmly with the ambitions of a left-wing populism. While theory and practice of democracy is not blameless in the causes and dynamics of right-wing populist resurgence, it is less democracy that is the problem than its liberal hollowing-out and capture. Indeed, in evaluating and diagnosing the current rise of right-wing populism, there can be little doubt that neoliberal policies have been a significant cause of social disaffection, economic inequality, and political alienation; these are the breeding grounds for right-wing populism. This neoliberal agenda has contrived to place democracy a poor second or third in the political race. In the process, "liberalism created the conditions and tools for the ascent of its own worst nightmare."[12] Consequently, the advance of a genuine and full-blooded democracy will require that populism is loosed from the soft shackles of liberalism and rescued from the eager clutches of a right-wing populism. Unlike both of those empty, if alluring clarion-calls, democracy can deliver on its anti-elitist, pluralist, and emancipatory ideals.

The Judicial Elite

In societies that are characterized by massive inequality of economic resources and, as a result, are governed by an economic-political elite, what does this suggest about the role and performance of the judiciary? Entrusted with the significant task of bringing meaning and effect to the constitution, they are placed in a very difficult and important position. Of course, the dominant constitutionalist view is that the courts can and do act as a bulwark against elitism; the professional development of constitutional law is considered to be detached from such powerful interests and, at its best, works to curb their influence and impact. However, there is little reason or facts on the ground to support such optimism; the practices and performances of the courts are very much within the elitist context of general and constitutional politics.[13] Nevertheless, there are many institutional aspects of the courts' workings and judges' approaches that reveal the close connection between the economic-political establishment and constitutional law. It is not only in politics that money talks; it also has a voice, albeit more modulated and discrete, in judicial circles.

Legal actions, constitutional or otherwise, are not a cheap affair. The costs of litigation are mainly economic, but they also have other less obvious costs, like psychological and social harms. But, even when viewed through a primarily economic and elitist lens, the challenges to ordinary people in bringing constitutional claims are extensive and imposing:

- *Personnel* – Judges do not represent a cross-section of society: they are appointed by the political elite (either the president or prime minister) and they are drawn from the professional ranks of lawyers. The socio-economic background of lawyers might well have been lowly to begin with, but they become, by virtue of being lawyers, part of or on the fringes of the economic and social elite. While there have been positive changes in the diversity of lawyers and the judiciary, the legal profession still remains a privileged class in terms of status, class, gender, race, religion, sexual orientation, and so on, and this affects its world view;
- *Fees and costs* – The costs of litigating are typically very large. While there are no prohibitive official fees charged for using the courts, the costs of lawyers are extremely high and out of the reach of most ordinary persons – taking a case to trial and beyond can amount to six-figure bills or higher. While there are some

initiatives to defray those costs (e.g., legal aid, pro bono, and cost-shifting), these are very much the exception, not the rule. It is not surprising, therefore that established and corporate interests tend to be the main and most numerous litigants, even in constitutional law. So privileged, they are able to influence the courts' agenda and the arguments that are made to them; and

- *Discourse* – Legal proceedings take place in a setting and vernacular that are alien and alienating to most people; legal doctrine and the procedural process are not easily accessible or understandable to the layperson. Also, trials and courts can be an intimidating venue for people who are unfamiliar with their rites and routines; it is an exclusionary and elite setting. Even when people win, they do not necessarily understand why or experience the desired sense of vindication. Insofar as justice is done, it is something that often occurs despite the involvement of people and complainants: it is more an act of legal *noblesse oblige* than anything else. In short, constitutional law is a world unto itself.

As such, there is a strong connection between the existence of economic inequality and the nature of constitutional law. Indeed, there is little about the legal process that is democratic in spirit, style, or substance. As the old saw goes, "Justice is open to everyone in the same way as the Ritz Hotel." No one is barred from entering or staying as long as you have the funds and the connections to get a booking. Once you are in, of course, you will be rubbing shoulders with other similarly situated people and talking in the way that they do; it is an exclusive club and that is a significant part of its appeal. For the democrat, none of this works in matters of accommodation, let alone the development of constitutional law and justice. If constitutional law is so important for and so essential to society, as the constitutionalists insist, then its central institutions must be accessible to ordinary people and be in line with their budgets. The way that it is presently arranged only serves to distance people from the very settings and contexts within which their rights and entitlements are determined and enforced. The democrat might be forgiven for thinking that it all amounts to an elaborate ruse in which justice, like so much else, is traded in a marketplace where only the favoured few can come to buy.

A glaring example of the failure of courts to address the unequal effects of wealth and class on social justice is the treatment of equality in constitutional law. In recent decades, there have been massive strides made in tackling a range of discriminatory dynamics in North America. The most conspicuous of these are, of course, the efforts to address and dismantle the pernicious effects of racism, sexism, and homophobia. While there is still a long way to go, much has been achieved. Nevertheless, mindful of the extent of economic inequality and the work of its deep dynamics in shaping social opportunities and outcomes, the unwillingness of the courts to include wealth as a "suspect category" of discrimination that judges can draw upon to inform equality jurisprudence is both troubling and revealing.[14] Without some acknowledgment of the role that wealth and its unequal distribution has upon social practices and institutions, including courts, constitutionalism will remain largely irrelevant to the vast underclass in modern society; it will help breed a problematic populism that disparages democracy as much as defends it.

Perhaps the most obvious example of this in constitutional law and doctrine is around so-called free speech in the United States. The Supreme Court's jurisprudence has taken a stance that consistently refuses to accept the all-too-cozy relation between politics and economics: "the concept that government may restrict the speech of some elements of our society in order to enhance the relative voice of others is wholly foreign to the First Amendment."[15] By ignoring the real-world impact of money and rejecting government's efforts to curb moneyed speech in the name of a more equal democratic dialogue, the courts have allowed the constitution to be used by the economic elite to advance their own interests; neutrality between corporate and popular speech is far from neutral in a world of dire inequality. Such a stance allows franchise and finance to become increasingly mutually dependent and reinforcing. Unfortunately, this trend reached its natural culmination in the dreadful decision of *Citizens United*: it was decided that restrictions on expenditures by corporations for the purposes

of political campaigning were unconstitutional. Apart from under-
lining rather than obscuring the ideological nature of judicial
decision-making, it is also a debilitating blow against democracy.
As the dissenting Justice Stevens put it, the ruling amounted to "a
rejection of the common sense of the American people, who have
recognized a need to prevent corporations from undermining self-
government."[16] Democracy is about people and participation, not
companies and profits.

Notwithstanding all this, the standing and reputation of courts
and judges remains very high in both Canada and United States.
Indeed, the constitution remains highly supported as does the
work of its judicial guardians; they fare so much better in the public
mind than the political process and politicians do. In the United
States, for instance, the Constitution in general (and presumably the judges) receive very high approval rating: only 1 per
cent of people believe that the Constitution should be scrapped
and redone. However, despite general faith in the Constitution,
almost 50 per cent insist that some changes need to be made, with
most of those not favouring major changes.[17] Although far from
unanimous, this general view is relied on by constitutionalists
and others to defend the courts and their centrality to constitutional law.

In Canada, the situation is not much different. In 2013, a Statistics Canada survey found that 93 per cent of Canadians saw
the Charter of Rights as being the most important of national
symbols: it received more support than the flag, the beaver, or
even hockey. It was also reported that more than 60 per cent
of Canadians were proud of the country's Constitution as a
whole.[18] This also combined with the fact that 90 per cent of
Canadians across the political spectrum maintained that they
have respect for Supreme Court Justices and their decisions,
even though they might not always agree with them (or even
know who they are). Significantly, as in the United States,
Canadians trusted their top court more than any other Canadian institution and certainly more than Parliament and other
legislative chambers.[19]

For the democrat, these are puzzling trends, at least on first sight.
However, rather than be viewed as representing a dissatisfaction

7.3 The perceived role of the Supreme Court

Thinking of these recent decisions, and the role of the Supreme Court generally, would you say the court has had a positive or negative effect on each of the following?

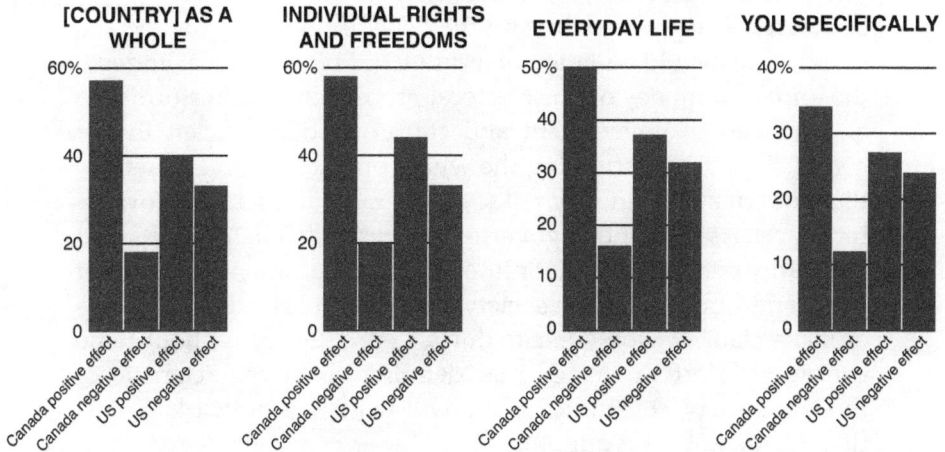

with democracy generally, it is more accurately understood as a continuing and deep discontent with the current state of democracy and the representative process. It is surely the case that a preference for courts and their legitimacy says as much about politics and politicians as it does about judges. On such terms, support for the Supreme Court is less an accolade for the work of judges and more a slap in the face for politicians. Moreover, there is no democratic logic for preferring the judges over the politicians in regard to procedural or substantive values; they are both elitist venues that tend to represent elitist interests and concerns. As has been said so well and so often, "We may grant until we're blue in the face that legislatures aren't wholly democratic, but that isn't going to make courts more democratic than legislatures."[20] Accordingly, a commitment to democracy demands that there should be a consistent and comprehensive rejection of elites: choosing between different elites is something of a Hobson's choice. On both counts, ordinary people are relegated to the role of passive listeners, at best, and not active participants in the governmental conversation. A judocracy is another form of elitism and should be rejected.

Conclusion

It seems beyond question that the operation of democracy and constitutionalism will not go untouched or unblemished by the existence of large inequalities in society. When there is such a gap between the moneyed elite and the general populace, democracy becomes an insipid imitation of its more full-blooded ideal. Indeed, the impact of money on the electoral process and the performance and policies of government and courts is so significant that it comes close to undermining the whole practice of government in the modern state – money talks, government listens, and government acts. As part of that governmental establishment, courts and judges are enmeshed in that plutocratic configuration; they are not as separate and apart from society's politics and elite machinations as many claim or would like to think. Consequently, without some concerted effort to change that defining elitist characteristic of modern society, constitutionalism will work as a bulwark against democracy, not in favour of it.

chapter eight

Towards "Democratic Courts": A Salvage Operation

The critique of the constitutionalist stance from a strongly democratic perspective, of course, is not new. Many scholars and jurists need little persuading that courts occupy an anomalous and disturbing position in a society and legal system that is supposed to be committed to a democratic imperative in both its organization and operation. Moreover, they accept that courts cannot achieve, no matter how hard they try or how principled their efforts, the guiding ambition of fulfilling their constitutionalist function in a way that is apolitical, neutral, high-minded, and objective: courts are inevitably and unavoidably engaged in an ideological endeavour, albeit in a more professional, polished, and more nuanced way than other governmental institutions and agencies. Nonetheless, these constitutionalist-friendly critics are not prepared to give up on the idea that it might be possible to retain presently constituted courts as constitutional arbiters and develop a practice of judicial decision-making that can square with the ideals of a thoroughly democratic mode of constitutional governance. As such, this small group of legal theorists recommend that judicial review is salvageable in that it can be done in a way that is both openly political and, at the same time, faithfully democratic in method and results.

All of these efforts can be considered innovative and valiant; they are driven by an honourable and democratic spirit. But, on closer scrutiny and read in their best light, they do more to ameliorate the effects of the democratic critique than overcome it: they sell democracy short as they claim to salvage it from the stifling grip of the traditionalist constitutionalists. Indeed, they might be guilty of the dubious sin of making the best of a very bad job. Furthermore, and somewhat ironically, although they strive to advance the democratic project by proposing that courts might be more directly and freely guided by the force and details of a democratic agenda, these jurists and commentators only serve to illuminate and reinforce the very problem that they are intended to resolve – courts, as presently organized and populated, are an impediment to a truly democratic and participatory system of political governance. Consequently, in this chapter, I will explore these pro-democracy or political accounts of judicial review and highlight their successes and failures. After looking at the efforts of various jurists, I will turn to the attempt by the courts to take onboard the democratic critique of "law as politics." Although each contribution is an improvement on more traditional approaches, they all still fail to live up to the demanding standards of their own critique and, particularly, of a truly democratic sensibility.

Demi-Democrats?

John Hart Ely is arguably the doyen of democratic jurists. His work to demonstrate that constitutional review by judges can be made to square with democratic governance has had a deservedly wide and deep appeal. Indeed, after the publication of *Democracy and Distrust*, it was difficult to do constitutional jurisprudence without taking a stand on his critical ideas and constructive proposals. He began by rejecting the work of jurists of all stripes – whether originalist, textualist, traditionalist, moralist or whatever – who sought to demonstrate that the work of courts could be done without taking a stand on controversial and contested political choices. Few can argue with the power and potency of that critique. However, he was not content with sweeping away the dubious feast of prevailing constitutionalist theories. Whether for strategic reasons (i.e., the Supreme Court was here to stay, so best offer a way for them to do their job better) or theoretical reasons (i.e., he really did believe that the Supreme Court was best placed to advance democracy),

Ely went on to offer his own account about how courts could fulfil their roles and responsibilities within a political system built on democratic commitments and demands.

For Ely, the primary and exclusive duty under the American Constitution was to police and unclog the processes of democratic decision-making. In confining themselves to this task, judges and jurists might be able to avoid the treacherous terrain of "substantive values" that was the burial ground of all previous accounts of judicial legitimacy. Accordingly, although far from obvious or beyond dispute, he insisted that the unenumerated rights of the Constitution, like the 14th Amendment's guarantee of equality or the 9th Amendment's protection of free speech, should be treated as being procedural safeguards, not substantive entitlements. For him, this might ensure that the political process – which is where such values are properly identified, weighted, and accommodated – "becomes open to those of all viewpoints on something approaching an equal basis."[1] In developing this idea, Ely relied upon the famous "footnote four" in *U.S. v. Carolene Products* – "legislation which restricts those political processes which can ordinarily be expected to bring about repeal of undesirable legislation is to be subjected to more exacting judicial prejudice against discrete and insular minorities may be a special condition, which tends seriously to curtail the operation of those political processes ordinarily to be relied upon to protect minorities, and which call for a more correspondingly more searching inquiry."[2] It was an inventive and enticing effort to bridge the apparent chasm between popular decision-making and the judicial implementation of law's constitutional mandates.

Ely's proposals were based more on good intentions than solid analysis (and everyone knows where that can lead). Not surprisingly, his work was met with serious criticisms and deep reservations. There were two particular arguments against Ely that spoke to the fragility of his constructive proposals in terms of their democratic pedigree. The first is that the difference between substance and procedure is not at all clear or undisputed. It is not so much that procedure has no value, rather that it has no value in and of itself. For procedures to be valued, they must lead to outcomes that are more conducive to the attainment or advancement of substantive values, like dignity, respect, or freedom. Moreover, in policing and protecting the wisdom or efficacy of any particular process, judges will have to make substantive assessments about the relative merits of competing political processes. Consequently, Ely finds himself back in the same place that he began and open to the same criticisms that he directed at other would-be constitutional jurists – the courts are no place to make contested and contestable choices among political values and principles if we are concerned about the priority and legitimacy of democratic governance.

The second and related argument against Ely's representative-reinforcing approach is that, while he takes the demands of democracy much more seriously than his traditional juristic colleagues, he fails to appreciate that there is more to democracy and popular participation than majoritarian decision-making through representative institutions and a distrust of judicial review. He allows "the people" to have the constitution they want, but does little more than identify "the people" as being synonymous with the legislature. Neglecting any actual participation by citizens in constitutional change, the tension between constitutionalism and democracy is attributed to the contested limits imposed by judicial review on the powers of a democratically elected legislature. This dichotomous approach to institutional supremacy (i.e., judicial or parliamentary/congressional) tends to reinforce the second-class status, at best, of popular participation and civic engagement. In short, Ely is unable to surmount or circumvent his own stricture that "society did not make the constitutional decision to move to near-universal suffrage only to turn round and have superimposed on popular decisions the values of first-rate lawyers."[3] As Ely might have assumed, the preference for process over substance is itself a political choice and goes to the heart of the traditional lawyers' mindset.

A later and Canadian effort to take an Elyian line and avoid the pitfalls that defeated Ely's own proposal is the work of Patrick Monahan. Monahan starts with the unabashed confession that "plainly, I regard [constitutional] interpretation as inherently and thoroughly political."[4] However, he maintains that it is still feasible to think about constructing a theory of judicial review that is suited not only to addressing the institutional dilemmas of democracy generally, but also to negotiating the practical predicaments of contemporary Canadian governance particularly. For him, therefore, this amounts to developing "a concept of judicial review that best fits the distinctive traditions of Canadian politics and society."[5] This is a tall order by any measure, but it is particularly lofty and rarified when it embraces what would be involved in offering an account that relies on this "distinctive tradition" as a means for resolving the more difficult and detailed challenges of constitutional meaning and application that present themselves to the courts. If it is to have any chance of success, this jurisprudential initiative will need to be as nuanced as it is robust.

Mindful of Ely's unconvincing distinction between process and substance, Monahan recommends that the best mode of constitutional review is one that gives primacy to the values of democracy and community. Crucially (and in contrast to Ely), he insists that this is an openly political undertaking that involves making substantive judgments, but one that can nevertheless be guided by the values of democracy and community themselves. For him, such an account offers the best fit with Canadian political and legal traditions. Of course, recognizing that both democracy and community are far from determinate and fixed in meaning or application, he remains confident that these lodestars can offer sufficient guidance to judges, even in high-profile and hard cases: the issue for the court is not "whether the court regarded those outcomes [of legislative decisions] as substantively just or right ... [but] whether the process which had produced the decision in question had conformed to democratic values." Monahan's guiding precept, therefore, is that judicial review should be viewed "as a mechanism to protect existing opportunities for democratic debate and dialogue as well as to open new avenues for such debate."[6]

This is stirring stuff and places the democratic project front and centre on the constitutional stage. However, despite its central and candid acceptance of judicial politics' inevitability, it falls victim to similar objections that beset any Elyian-inspired intervention. In particular, Monahan is unable to surmount the crucial issue of why courts would be better suited and more legitimate than legislatures

(or any other and more democratic body) at determining the best substantive choices to be made, especially about political processes and
communal values. When he states that "constitutional argument ...
should be limited to the narrow issue of whether the means chosen
by government to achieve ... important objective[s] is unduly restrictive of other social values,"[7] he offers no reason about how judges'
handling of this balancing of values should take priority over that
of the legislature or executive branch of government. Indeed, his
invocation of "constitutional argument" as something different to
non-constitutional argument seems to resurrect the much-maligned
notion of legal argument as having a distinct identity from ideological argument. As Ely himself memorably noted, "We may grant until
we're blue in the face that legislatures aren't wholly democratic, but
that isn't going to make courts more democratic than legislatures."[8]
If constitutional law is politics, then there seems even less reason for
presently constituted courts to be involved.

The shared problem of Ely and Monahan is that, having recognized
that courts have a definite deficit in terms of democratic legitimacy,
they are unable to explain why a coterie of elite bureaucrats –
as opposed to citizens and the political community more broadly –
should be entrusted with the privilege of having the last word on
constitutional and, therefore, political matters. This is especially
the case when it is conceded, as Monahan does, that there is no
special mode of legal or constitutional argument that is separate or
different from political debate. If that is so (and I strongly maintain
that it is), there is a need for a much more radical and far-reaching
set of changes in the structure of courts, the identity of judges, and
their operating protocols. These demi-democrats are, as their name
suggests, half-hearted in their willingness to follow through on the
institutional implications of a strong democratic critique. A more
extensive and disruptive program of reforms is needed.[9]

Throwing in the Towel?

There is one more popular response to the finding that constitutional
doctrine and argument is thoroughly ideological and unavoidably

so. Moreover, its adherents eschew the effort to develop any account or theory of constitutional adjudication that offers some overarching methodology, whether moral, political, or democratic, that judges can utilize to overcome or sidestep the democratic deficit. Instead, what they recommend is that judges take a pragmatic and incrementalist approach to their constitutional duties. Situating themselves between the discredited formalist and the cynical critic,[10] they insist that, while there is an inescapable ideological element to judicial decision-making, law can place constraints on what would otherwise be an open-ended exercise of political judgment. In an important sense, they want to have their traditional constitutionalist cake and eat it too.

One of those pragmatists is Richard Fallon. For him, it is not theoretical purity or historical fidelity that controls, but more that prudence and pragmatism are necessary dimensions of judicial decision-making that should be nurtured, not ignored or hidden. He recommends that judges can best achieve that goal by drawing upon established traditions of argument and reasoning that lead to objective and principled standards that shape and structure but do not determine legal judgment. As such, "the justices' core mission involves the provision of reasoned justice under law" that "they advance in good faith." Fallon goes on to say that, although there is always room for legal disagreement, there is much that is untenable and unreasonable: disagreement among judges and jurists is acceptable and inevitable as long as it is "reasonable." Accordingly, for him, judges judge best when they combine the consistent application of sound interpretive principles with robust convictions about the substantive force of constitutional commitments. He makes no calls for radical change or widespread reappraisals, but he does recommend that judicial appointments should be more centrist and that judges should "exhibit greater restraint."[11] It is on all fronts a modest and middle-of-the-road account of what constitutional judging is and ought to be about.

Another figure in the pragmatist camp is Cass Sunstein. Sunstein offers a minimalist account of constitutional adjudication by arguing that the most appropriate and efficacious way for judges to proceed is to "speak softly and carry a small stick." Insisting that there is no single surefire way to elicit constitutional meaning, he contends that the most appropriate interpretive approach depends on what will make the constitutional system "better than worse." In the American context, this means that judges and jurists must defend their interpretive preferences and decisions in terms of fulfilling both the institutional and substantive demands on judges in a republican system of constitutional democracy. For him, the minimalists' belief that "small steps are often the right steps" is the safest and surest way forward as it avoids dangerous leaps in the political dark. As such, he celebrates the "integrity and coherence" of both legal and social traditions as revealed in the history of American constitutional thought. However, while he is traditional on institutional matters (e.g., separation of powers and national security), he is less so when it comes to individual rights (e.g., race, sex, disability) because there are more compelling reasons for "traditions to be held to account."[12] But, even when judges challenge traditions (as part of the constitutional tradition itself), they must do so in a minimalist way such that legal precedent and social traditions are destabilized as little as possible. As such, Sunstein's constitutional minimalism calls upon the common-law tradition of incrementalism in matters of law and social change.

These modest pragmatists have, as Winston Churchill said of a political rival, much to be modest about. Their account of constitutional judging fails both descriptively and prescriptively. As a descriptive account, their emphasis on small and modest steps fails to explain the pattern and development of constitutional doctrine. Law does not develop in small steps but is marked by a series of "great cases" that work to push forward doctrine in large, nontraditional, and often revolutionary ways; *Brown* and *Roe* in the United States and *Fraser* and *Carter* in Canada are not the immodest stuff of incremental change.[13] As a prescriptive account, pragmatism fails because, in recommending that judges take small and modest steps, it says nothing about the direction that any steps should or should not be taken in. Even a minimalist has to be minimalist about something; there is no self-contained ethic or political standard in the plea to be minimalist. As such, a pragmatic approach has no basis at all from which to propose why being minimally progressive is better or worse than being minimally conservative.

From a democratic standpoint, a minimalist and modest account of constitutional judging has to be able to demonstrate that, as Fallon puts it, it is not "so flaccid that [it] will permit the justices, with five votes, to do anything that they might be able to get away with."[14] However, despite their protestations to the contrary, even though they accept that constitutional law has an inescapable ideological element, their accounts are shaved so thin as to place no real or worthwhile constraints on judges. Provided judges act in good faith and offer reasoned arguments, they are largely undisciplined and can do almost whatever they wish. After all, if the judgments and decisions of Justices Scalia and Thomas as well as Justices Marshall and Ginsberg are each and all legitimate, then the alleged constraints of their proposed approach are doing very little work. This means that an elite group, like Supreme Court judges, gets to tell the citizenry what to do in line with their own, not society's political morality (or, at best, their own view of what society's political morality is). Indeed, this almost laissez-faire approach to the importance of judges' substantive convictions merely serves to compound the already tenuous legitimacy of the traditional constitutionalist model.

All of this amounts to more of a throwing in the towel than providing a workable response to the courts' political and undemocratic role. The injunction for judges to "be reasonable" is not so much a plea to be apolitical but an effort to disguise middle-of-the-road moderation as being somehow non-political in nature. Theirs is a thinly veiled apology for the status quo until, of course, the status quo changes; today's moderate is yesterday's radical and tomorrow's conservative. While these pragmatists claim to affect a reasonable pose, they have little to offer the democrat other than a patronizing reassurance that, as long as judges write like judges, be honest, and follow their political instincts, all will be fine because they will not stray far from the political mainstream. This is, at best, an act of *noblesse oblige* that does as much to deflect and undermine a genuine commitment as other grander and more substantive theories of judicial review. The political mainstream is no less political than the more extreme locations along the political spectrum.

Democratic Dialogue

In Canada, the advent of the Charter crystallized the long-standing dilemma of the courts in trying to reconcile their new role as active guardians of fundamental values with the democratic values and traditions of Canadian society. They had to develop a way to act decisively as well as legitimately. In the Charter's early years, judges relied upon the old standby of "liberal legalism" – a sharp public/private distinction, neutral interpretation, and objective balancing – as a method for legitimizing their decisions and reconciling the courts' role with democracy. However, it soon became clear that this jurisprudential methodology was failing to placate either liberal or more radical critics who complained that judicial review was not fulfilling its functions as effectively or as democratically as it might. Not only were the courts' efforts at preserving a sharp distinction between legal analysis and political judgment becoming more threadbare and unconvincing, but also the substantive political values that animated their decisions were being revealed as increasingly outdated and unresponsive to contemporary Canadian sensibilities. Indeed, "liberal legalism" was unable to command a sustained consensus even amongst judges.

In response, the Supreme Court began to nurture a less legalistic and more pragmatic approach to its constitutional duties. The Supreme Court did modify and mollify its approach in light of these criticisms, especially in its approach to equality (abandoning the old Bill of Rights approach) and to the reach of the Charter under section 32 (rejecting unsustainable distinctions). Moreover, the general thrust of the law-is-politics critique was heeded to the limited extent that the courts backed off from a transparent and discredited version of "legal formalism" that pretended that constitutional law was simply a matter of interpretive conformity with no connection to wider debates about national values and social policies. Protestations about simply being involved in a technical interpretation of relevant textual provisions became much less frequent. Ironically, these very efforts to bolster their democratic legitimacy by relying upon an apparently more overt mode of

democratic justification revealed even more starkly how undemocratic the judges' involvement in judicial review under the Charter
was.[15]

In recent years, there has been a turn to "dialogue theory" as
an alternative justification for judicial review. Judges and jurists
have begun to accept that some reliance upon contested political
commitments is not only inevitable but also desirable. The primary concern is less with politicization itself and more with "the
degree to which judges are free to read their own preferences into
law."[16] As such, judicial activism is less about whether judges rely
on political preferences at all and more about the sources of such
values and the extent to which they rely on them. Cautioning that
judges are not free to go wherever their personal political preferences take them, the dialogic approach does not altogether abandon the idea or practice of maintaining a barrier between legitimate
legal analysis and illegitimate political decision-making. Instead,
it is argued that the distinction is much fuzzier, that the domain
of law is much more expansive, and that the boundary between
law and politics is much less breached. However, as part of their
general constitutionalist orientation, they conceded that there
is a point at which the judges can be said to be no longer doing
law; they will have wandered off into other parts of the constitutional and political domain. In some important sense, law was still
understood to exist separately from its judicial spokesperson such
that law places some non-trivial constraints on what judges can
do and say. Although admitting that legal principles were more
open and sensitive to political context, they remained convinced
that law is not only reduced to the contingent political preferences
of the judiciary.

Consequently, the general thrust of the dialogue theory was that,
because the legislature possesses the final word on Charter matters
by virtue of the section 33 override power, the courts can proceed
to engage in a more overt balancing of political values under section 1's "reasonable limits" provision. The claim and hope was
that the courts and the legislature would engage in an institutional
conversation about the Charter and its requirements on particular
and pressing issues of the day: the courts and the legislators have

complementary roles that enable legislation to be carefully tailored to meet the government's political agenda and respect Charter values. The most prominent judicial advocate of a dialogic approach was Justice Iacobucci who insisted that "judicial review on Charter grounds brings a certain measure of vitality to the democratic process, in that it fosters both dynamic interaction and accountability amongst the various branches."[17] In establishing a "dialogic balance" and "retaining a forum for dialogue" between the different branches of government, the courts must tread a thin but vital line between deferential subservience and robust activism. The courts and legislatures are to be dialogic partners in an institutional conversation to advance shared democratic goals.

This resort to "democratic dialogue" does at least concede the normative nature of Charter decision-making and represent an effort to get beyond a discredited notion of liberal legalism; it seems to have let the political cat out of the judicial bag without any plan for getting it back in or keeping it suitably leashed. The majority judgments in *Doucet* offer compelling evidence of this claim. Indeed, suspiciously bereft of any reference to "dialogic theory," the judgment of Justices Iacobucci and Arbour spends much of its time, directly and indirectly, trying to repel the debilitating spectre of judicial activism. Although the majority emphasize time and again that "courts must ensure that government behaviour conforms with constitutional norms but in doing so must also be sensitive to the separation of function among the legislative, judicial and executive branches," they are relatively quiet on how that separation is to be achieved. Eschewing the notion that there is some "bright line" in existence, their only serious suggestion is that judges must be thoroughly pragmatic and contextual in their assessments: "determining the boundaries of the courts' proper role, however, cannot be reduced to a simple test or formula; it will vary according to the right at issue and the context of each case."[18] The conclusion that the judicial approach to remedies must remain flexible and responsive to the needs of a given case is unlikely to give comfort to those critics who look for some discipline in or direction to the courts' future performance. An uncommitted observer might be forgiven for thinking that, on the question of whether "law is politics," the court has given up the ghost rather than exorcised the wraith of judicial activism.

Accordingly, with its apparent rejection of judicial objectivity, lack of normative content, and vague invocations of democracy, the most recent juristic approaches to judicial review actually serve to undermine fatally the project of justifying constitutional adjudication's democratic legitimacy. Although dialogic theory is intended to calm fears that the courts are undisciplined and unlimited in their powers, it manages to reinforce the perception that courts are not only at the centre of the crucial process through which political discourse and values are shaped and sustained, but also that courts get to determine the role and contribution of the other branches of government.[19] The "degree to which judges are free to read their own preferences into law" seems to be reducible to the rather oxymoronic conclusion that they will be as "free to read their own preferences into the law" as "their own preferences" allow. As such, there is a huge gap between the rhetoric of democratic dialogue and the reality of judicial performance. Presenting judicial review as part and parcel of a democratic dialogue merely underlines the extent to which democracy has become a caricature of itself. An elite and stilted conversation between the judicial and executive branches of government is an entirely impoverished performance of democracy; it is an empty echo of what should be a more resounding commotion.

Against Supremacy

In many ways, the demi-democrats, pragmatists, and dialogists fall foul of Benjamin Disraeli's sage political advice – "the most dangerous strategy is to jump a chasm in two leaps." Although they take the important first step of illuminating the political character of legal argument and the anti-democratic nature of judicial review, they pause in mid-jump and lose critical steam. So paused, they propose a second step by recommending a way to make good on the democratic deficit by suggesting a way that judges can do what they do, but in a more democratic way. This is a very odd and unconvincing manoeuvre; it is destined to result in theoretical disaster. However, there is one other group of scholars who are unrelenting in their commitment to the political-democratic critique – the anti-supremacists. Perhaps for felt reasons of strategic necessity (e.g., no foreseeable demise of the Supreme Court in the near or mid-term), they work towards overcoming the supremacy of judicial review as a tool of constitutional interpretation, but not abandoning it entirely. Instead, they explore other sources and sites of popular involvement in constitutional governance.

One leading practitioner of this popular constitutionalism is Larry Kramer. Relying on a rigorous historical analysis, he defends the compelling thesis that the American constitutional arrangement was not originally based on the notion of judicial supremacy but on the idea and practice of popular sovereignty and customary practice: "against the larger backdrop of American history, the acceptance of judicial supremacy in modern constitutional times is anomalous." Contrary to contemporary understandings, he insists that the Constitution was intended to be a document that could and should be interpreted by the people and be remade at any time by the people; the supremacy of the Supreme Court was not at all in the founders' minds. As the years have passed by, Kramer shows how the collapse or debasement of democratic politics has worked to reinforce and insulate the central power and authority of the courts and judicial review. For him, judges and jurists have hijacked the Constitution and, in the process, been aided and abetted by the political elite: "supporters of judicial supremacy are today's aristocracy."[20]

This is a powerful narrative that seeks to restore the centrality of democracy and popular sovereignty to the historical arc of American constitutionalism. Strong democrats have much to learn from Kramer and the sources that he relies on. However, he is not as compelling or as reassuring when it comes to what can be done today to reorient and redress the current imbalance. He hedges his bets and, in doing so, loses much of his emancipatory influence. Still retaining some belief in the romanticized traditional account of lawyers as progressive activists and thinkers, he is reluctant to recommend, let alone campaign for, the abandonment of the Supreme Court as presently constituted. While he recommends that it should not have the final say in constitutional matters, he offers no sustained ideas about what adjustments would be necessary. Instead, he concludes with the recognition that people have to learn "to live with the jerry-built system of accountability that evolved."[21] Unfortunately, this resigned plea is born more of hope than conviction. For all the fierce wisdom of his analytical critique, Kramer seems to lack the political will to do what the American founders did – take history by the scruff of its neck and make it bend to the will of the people (or, in their case, its elite factions).

A more robust and uncompromising stance is taken by Mark Tushnet. More political and less historical than Kramer, he offers a *tour de force* of the popular constitutionalist mandate. For him, to be pro-constitution is not to be anti-democratic: it is courts and judicial review that are the problem, not the constitution. Accordingly, although he rejects judicial supremacy, he does not dismiss the importance of rights or their need for constitutional protection. With a keen sensitivity to the demands of both a critical and democratic imperative, he explores how constitutional law might be wrested from the suffocating grip of the Supreme Court, distributed to other institutional venues, and handed back to the people: "all constitutional provisions are up for grabs at all times."[22] To effect his position, he draws a significant distinction between a thick and thin Constitution. Whereas the thick version comprises all the provisions and jurisprudence of the full constitutional materials, the thin version is stripped down to the essential principles of the Declaration of Independence – "We hold these truths to be self-evident, that all men are created equal, that they are endowed by their Creator with certain unalienable Rights, that among these are Life, Liberty and the pursuit of Happiness. – That to secure these rights, Governments are instituted among Men, deriving their just powers from the consent of the governed." In blunt terms, the thick Constitution is derivative and dependent on the thin Constitution.

On the basis of this, Tushnet maintains that "the project for populist constitutional law is to continue and extend the narrative of the thin Constitution." This is done by striving to "restyle ... the Constitution around ... the Declaration's principles" and by taking this task and, therefore, "constitutional law away from the courts."[23] In this way, he claims that the thin Constitution can provide a framework for addressing political controversies, but not dictate or determine any particular outcomes. Differing from Justice Jackson's famous quip, Tushnet believes that the Supreme Court is neither final nor infallible.[24] Instead, he contends that what Supreme Court judges have to say is important, but it is not definitive or authoritative by that fact alone. There are other sites – Congress, agencies, presidents, departments, and so on – that can allow non-professionals and non-elites to offer their own interpretations and applications of the thin Constitution's principles. Nothing is guaranteed by way of outcome or result; the constitutional debate will be popular and broad, but it will not be fixed or conclusive. Consequently, Tushnet seeks to multiply the sites that society relies upon to generate constitutional meaning and through which people govern themselves.

There is so much in Tushnet's work that resonates with my own agenda of strong democracy. Indeed, his ideas and proposals are an effective bridge into my own proposals for institutional reform and realignment; much that I recommend is influenced by Tushnet's provocative version of popular constitutionalism. However, while he is marvellously suggestive and innovative in proposing ways that might advance his own project, he is a little short on how such a transformation can occur from an institutional and political perspective. Although he encourages the process of amendment, he leaves it to "able political leaders" to nurture and kindle people's participatory instincts in the constitutional project.[25] More pertinently, he still sees a possible role for an unreconstructed Supreme Court in developing and contributing to constitutional discourse. In modest contrast, I intend to explore more fully the ways in which citizens can more directly and frequently engage in the crucial democratic task of governing themselves. It is people and not institutions that must be at the heart of the democratic project.

Conclusion

Each of these theorists – demi-democrats, pragmatists, dialogists, and anti-supremacists – are a vast improvement on the more traditional juristic offerings. They offer a rich spread of criticisms and proposals that rely on and stimulate the democratic imagination. However, while they point in the right direction, they stop well short of their avowed democratic destination. In some ways, they still remain within the land and boundaries of the traditional strong constitutionalists, albeit on its outskirts. Of course, for the anti-supremacist, this is more a strategic concession than a principled recommendation; they reluctantly accept that truly transformative change is unlikely and that there is a need to work within certain existing constitutional parameters. Although I am sensitive to such a stance, I nevertheless maintain that strong democrats must have the courage of their convictions and break out into new territory where democracy is not subordinate to elites and non-participatory modes of constitutional creation and interpretation. Without some vision of what a genuinely and strongly democratic vision of constitutionalism might look like and what its institutional structure might be, there seems even less hope of a serious challenge to the constitutionalist status quo.

chapter nine

Beyond Courts:
Towards Democratic Institutions

The critique of the constitutionalist stance from a strongly democratic perspective, of course, does not in itself recommend any future course of action or scheme of government. In particular, the rejection of courts both as a supposedly professional and non-political forum for the resolution of contested matters of constitutional interpretation and as the indirect route for informal amendment is a no-brainer in terms of improved democratic performance and legitimacy. But this stance does not suggest how to take up the institutional slack left by the abandonment of courts. There remains the need to deal with some of the work that courts presently do in resolving focused and party-driven disputes and in giving specific meaning to general constitutional provisions. There is clearly some warrant for such a forum to deal with that important work. The fact that courts fail at those assignments does not mean that some other institutional agency is not needed or would also fail. Consequently, the challenge is to propose an alternative forum that would do the work of courts, without falling foul of the democratic critique that so easily skewers them in their traditional constitutionalist format and workings. Such an agency would need to be both democratic in orientation, democratic in membership, and democratic in performance. This is a tall order, but not one that is beyond the ken of the strong democrat.

In this chapter, therefore, I undertake the crucial (and some might say make-or-break) task of proposing an institution that fulfils the same constitutional functions as courts presently do, but not in a constitutionalist way. The challenge is to design an institution and suitable *modus operandi* for it that is not only acceptable to a democratic style of thinking but also advances the institutional dimension of the democratic project. Accordingly, in the first part, I summarize how courts fail and thereby make clear the pitfalls that must be avoided by any alternative forum. Secondly, I emphasize how any political process must measure itself in terms of the democratic outcome that it produces and the legitimacy that it claims. In the third part, I introduce the idea of a constitutional jury as a replacement for courts as the primary interpreters of the constitution. Finally, in the fourth part, I look at some of the practical difficulties that constitutional juries will have to confront and resolve in order to meet democratic expectations. Throughout the chapter, my overall ambition is to demonstrate that, in a democracy, political debate is something to be embraced, not rejected or modified, if constitutions are to be taken seriously.

How Courts Fail

The basic conceit at the heart of the constitutionalist endeavour is the claim that courts can be neutral and unaligned agencies of governance in fulfilling their task of interpreting and enforcing the constitution. But this is simply not the case. Jurists and judges have no cogent or convincing response to the central dilemma of the constitutionalist approach – *if the judiciary are by background much less representative of the public at large and by design much less accountable to the public at large, why should they be entitled to pass judgment on the important decisions and actions of governing legislative bodies, who are both more representative and more accountable?*[1] At bottom, the constitutionalist response comes down to the unedifying and self-serving notion that the judiciary's very unaccountability and unrepresentativeness actually works to ensure that fundamental and contested matters of political justice are addressed and resolved in an impartial, detached, and principled way.

As I have sought to demonstrate throughout this book, this response fails in so many ways: it relies on a large dose of angelic laughter and institutional forgetting to gain any traction. More-over, it manages to emphasize the wrong-headedness of such a stance that only serves to persuade and advance the interest of those elites, including the legal community broadly, who are already predisposed to accept it. There are three crucial and mis-taken assumptions that underlie this constitutionalist stance:

- *That fundamental and contested matters of political justice can be addressed and resolved in an impartial and principled way* – Even a rudimentary grasp of both history and philosophy indicates that any definitive and objective resolution has proved to be entirely elusive to all and sundry. If there is any consensus among historians and thinkers, it is that what counts as political justice at any particular time is irreducibly contested and controversial;
- *That courts can perform that task* – There is nothing in the history of constitutional adjudication that would warrant that such a conclusion was more defensible in the courts as opposed to anywhere else; vague trends and short-lived tendencies in constitutional doctrine are nothing more than that. The judicial parts are so much less than the sum of the constitutionalist whole; and
- *That legislatures and the executive do not do that* – While legislatures have no greater insight than courts or anyone else on resolving matters between competing visions of political justice, there is no evidence that legislatures do a worse job at it. Despite regular lapses, legislatures do no worse a job than courts and do not have added baggage of pretending to be following some artificial legal reason or constitutional logic.

Accordingly, any effort to move forward the debate about democracy and constitutions must begin with the indisputable acknowledgment that judges are unable to fulfil their constitu-tional responsibilities without resorting to and engaging with a range of contested and ideological issues. Theirs is a thoroughly and unavoidably political undertaking. This is particularly appar-ent when the historical arc of changing legal doctrine is examined and understood. Despite the valiant efforts of some democratically inspired jurists, there is no theory that can save judges from their political selves. If democracy is to be the guide and benchmark for constitutional governance, then the centrality and importance of courts in the political scheme of things must be rejected; judicial review disenfranchises citizens. Whether evaluated in terms of process or outcomes, courts fail to meet their self-imposed challenge. Indeed, it has become acceptable to state that "resisting popular views about the meaning of the Constitution is considered a judicial virtue."[2] Moreover, even if there were to be a democratically made Constitution, it is vital to interpret and apply it through democratic institutions and in a democratic way. Consequently, new ways of thinking about the interpretation and enforcement of constitutional rules need to be explored and introduced from a strongly democratic perspective.

One response is to make courts themselves more democratic. By that, it is meant that courts would still assume the primary responsibility of dealing with the constitution, but its judicial membership would be more democratic. For example, some critics have argued that reforms such as installing a more diverse judiciary, developing a career judiciary, introducing parliamentary oversight of judicial appointments and performance, and even election of judges would help to give greater democratic legitimacy to the process. Also, it will likely open up the elite ranks of the judicial and legal profession to groups of citizens – women, visible minorities, and others – who are currently excluded or, at least underrepresented. Moreover, while there are no guarantees, the increased involvement of these presently excluded persons will increase the likelihood of there being different interests being represented in the exercise of constitutional interpretation and judgment. Such robust dialogue is more conducive to the democratic temperament and civic advancement than the insulated monologues of legal professionals. However, even with such reforms (that would amount to an improvement on the status quo), this alternative remains too anchored in the constitutionalist vision and thus would only change the appearance, not the reality of judicial supremacy.[3] Indeed, the dangers of such reforms would be that they suggest greater success than they actually achieve. It would be throwing good money after bad. As long as such judges feel compelled and claim to be following some artificial professional reason or constitutional logic, it would be the non-democratic business-as-usual for all intents and purposes.

Another response has been to recommend a weaker form of judicial review. Insofar as I understand this proposal, it recommends that judicial review still continues as it does today in much the same way as constitutionalists recommend, but the resulting decisions are no longer supreme and are subject to legislative reconsideration.[4] This is clearly a significant improvement over existing models and practices of judicial review; it makes legislatures, not courts, the final arbiters of constitutional meaning and effect. However, there is only so much courts can or should do in this process. The proposal for "weak" judicial review only goes half the way to creating a truly democratic situation; it risks an institutional mixture that is the worst of both judicial and legislative action. As long as courts are viewed as speaking with an authoritative and non-political voice, albeit falsely so, it will be difficult for legislatures to claim a more convincing rationale for their own interventions and opinions. The defence of the "weak" review position perpetuates the mistaken idea that deep-seated political disagreements can be resolved by reference to technical and professional methods of inquiry and interpretation. Strong democrats reject such a possibility. Because they have the constitutional courage of their political convictions, democrats will not rely on such intellectual makeweights. Instead, they will deal with politics as a practical art, not a pseudoscientific enterprise. Consequently, the force of the democrats' critique of presently constituted courts demands their complete abandonment, not their partial curtailment.

Politics and Process

The only genuinely democratic response is to abandon any reliance on courts as presently constituted or in a future reformed format. That being said, the choice is not necessarily between courts as they presently exist and a vacuum. As a democrat, I do accept that it might be wise and practical for there to be some tribunal or body that is tasked with fulfilling the responsibilities that are presently undertaken by courts. In this, I largely agree with Frank Michelman's telling observation that "ultimate standards of fundamental-legal rightness cannot be left to democracy to decide, and that some official organ or organs have to be authorized to decide and construe from time to time the content of the fundamental laws."[5] But this does not mean by any stretch that such a vital task should or must fall to courts and judges. While a multiplicity of deliberative institutions can play a useful role in a democratic polity, there is no reason at all why judicial review, as presently constituted, should be one of them. And, of course, I have suggested many reasons why it should not be.

In line with other democratic efforts, there should be many more sites at which citizens can directly and strongly participate in politics generally, including even constitutional ones. In particular, on questions of constitutional meaning, it is people's entitlement and responsibility as citizens to do so. Any group entrusted to interpret the Constitution must itself have a democratic pedigree (i.e., appointment and personnel) and strive to be democratic in its decision-making (i.e., process and substance). In fulfilling this mandate, the task is most definitely not to purge intellectual inquiry and debate of its political-ness as those traditional jurists who defend a continuing and central reliance on judicial review recommend. Instead, mindful that power can also be constitutive and enabling as well as restrictive and distorting, a democratic approach can meet power's challenge. It can organize democratic arrangements so as not only to maximize people's life choices and lifestyles but also to provide a set of communal resources through which the bases for these choices and styles can be debated and criticized. It is the strength of strong democracy that it can provide a process for debating and deciding upon political means and ends in a contingent way that claims no objective or analytical privilege. This might entail a commitment to devolve and diffuse power as much as practicably possible by fostering multiple forums for political engagement.

To revamp the whole system of legislative and executive processes in line with greater and more extensive popular participation will require a monumental effort. Moreover, any changes that are proposed – proportional representation, recall legislation, accountability audits, genuine ministerial responsibility, referenda, and so on – must themselves be legitimate products of the very democratic process that is to be enhanced. There are no easy solutions to the current undemocratic trends. In this sense, the debate around judicial review is something of a distraction. Improvement in society's democratic status will not come from increased interventions by judges in governmental policies. Indeed, judicial supervision is a short-term crutch that might actually harm a limping polity in the medium- and long-term march towards a fuller and stronger democracy. The replacement of one elite rule (executive or legislative) by another (judicial) can only be considered positive under the most warped sense of democracy.

So, if there is a desire to reign in the judges, there must also be a commitment to ensuring that elected politicians and officials are living up to their own demanding democratic responsibilities. At present, they are palpably not doing so. It is incumbent on politicians and officials to transform their own practices and performances in line with a more demanding sense of what being democratic entails. Simply construing the democratic challenge as being strictly about whether the judges stay out of or stray onto the political terrain is to misrepresent the problem and, therefore, hamper any genuine solutions. In line with this commitment, strong democrats will look to extend and proliferate the opportunities for participation in micro-communities: there is little to be gained by narrowing and accreting decision-making power to small and centralized elites in the name of expertise and truth.

This institutional transformation will involve two important initiatives in relation to existing arrangements. First, it will be important to reinvigorate democratically those bodies and organs (e.g., legislatures, municipalities, state agencies) that presently claim to be the decisive seat of democratic government. Rather than function as remote entities that have a tenuous claim to democratic legitimacy through occasional elections, they might begin to be less entrenched in their connections and more responsive in their deliberations and decisions; local government would replace federal and provincial government at the heart of democratic involvement. Tellingly, in American terms, "congress" might begin to approximate more closely to its original meaning as "a gathering of people" and, in Anglo-Canadian terms, "parliament" might more closely resemble its roots in "a place for debate." Representation and participation could become less structured and more popular in action and ambition.

Second, it will be important to ensure that the number of democratic bodies that exist and the occasions on which they are utilized will develop and increase: more people participating more often is a measure of the political system's democratic vigour and commitment. However, if there is to be a spread of second-, third- or even fourth-look bodies that contribute to the composition and implementation of policymaking, such institutions will themselves need to be more participatory; they will also need to be more directly accountable to popular views. Of course, judicial review does not meet such standards; appointed (and even elected) judges tend to operate in the same calcified and elitist ways as the elected legislatures that they are supposed to check. Contrary to the prevailing constitutionalist mindset, judges and politicians are drawn from similar elite sources. Accordingly, it will be necessary to engage citizens directly in more imaginative and participatory ways within such deliberative and policymaking bodies.

Revisiting Juries

Even with a vastly increased scheme of popular participation, conflict and disagreement will still occur. It is hopelessly naive to pretend that any system of governance, including and especially strong democracy, will be based on complete and lasting consensus; the appeal of strong democracy is that it will foster, not inhibit a pluralist culture of political engagement and this will inevitably generate contention.[6] Under such circumstances, the role of these multiple forums will not be to replicate courts and mimic the judicial (and juristic) preoccupation with establishing neutral and non-political bases for legitimating their actions. Instead, it might be accepted that, once there is a genuine and widespread practice of strong democracy, all bodies and agencies will be involved in the same game, namely delivering substantive answers to concrete problems. In doing so, while no one institution will have a lock on political judgment about what is the best thing to do, all institutions' decisions will be evaluated in terms of the value choices that they make and the contribution that their decisions make to advancing substantive democracy in the here and now. Accordingly, the appropriate inquiry in a strong democracy is not to ask whether particular policymaking bodies have acted politically and, therefore, improperly, but whether the political choices that they have made serve that society's democratic agenda. Because this democratic assessment is a substantive and political task, not a formal and analytical undertaking, it will always be a contested and contestable issue.

The purpose of increasing the number of sites available for popular involvement by citizens is to incorporate a broader range of voices that will be heard in society's continuing dialogue about the kind of democratic society it wishes to become. The central importance of this popular participation in shaping public values can only be grasped by focusing on institutions that reject values of expertise and elitism in favour of those of hands-on involvement and self-government by citizens. There already exist such forums in the existing legal process – the jury system. Although a proposal to extend its use and to multiply its sites runs counter to much received constitutionalist-influenced wisdom, especially in regard to constitutional review, this is no reason to be shy in efforts to strengthen juries in the name of democratic legitimacy. Indeed, some might say that the scepticism of the constitutionalist elite towards juries might well be a strong justification to promote its expanded role in legal and constitutional matters in a society that is fully and strongly committed to democracy.

The value and legitimacy of the jury has always been contested. For some, it is a democratic beacon that preserves popular participation in the remote and bureaucratized administration of justice; the tendency to sideline its use is, therefore, to be forcefully resisted. For others, it is a dubious institution that casts a long shadow of rank and popular prejudice over curial affairs. Indeed, critics on both the political right and left have condemned the jury as a vehicle for bigotry, ignorance, and worse. However, these criticisms of the jury parallel those made against democratic governance and popular participation in general. The basic complaint is that untrained individuals are ill-suited for making such important decisions in the life of the polity and its members. Yet, whatever the failings of individual juries might be (and they obviously exist), the jury system as a whole embodies to a remarkable degree the values of self-government by the citizenry at large. Through juries, people become institutional players in organizing their political and social lives rather than mere spectators of a governmental spectacle. Rejecting rule by experts, juries enable people to assume responsibility for making important civic decisions on a rotating basis. Because juries are expected to arrive at a common verdict through persuasion and argument, people's involvement will prioritize the democratic virtues of debate and engagement in a micro-setting. In contrast to judicial review, it will give the lie to the prevailing constitutionalist idea that "resisting popular views about the meaning of the Constitution is considered a [judicial] virtue."[7]

As an occasion for democratic devolution, jury empowerment would bring a neglected challenge to the aristocratic instincts of legal professionalism and might even invigorate the style, range, and direction of constitutional decision-making. By changing the civic members of the jury from passive observers to active participants, the process of constitutional interpretation might begin to meet democratic expectations. Because constitutional enforcement is a practical and political activity, it is too important to be left solely to lawyers. Moreover, by withdrawing the constitutional fate of the polity from the clutches of lawyers and jurists, it might become possible for citizens to overcome the dispiriting belief that without something large, powerful, and ahistorical on their side to support their claims – like "the law" – they need not assert their right to govern themselves. Accordingly, a revitalized jury system would help to relieve the symptoms of democratic ennui and prevent further political disempowerment. Viewed in this way, the jury system represents a commitment to the principle that ordinary citizens are capable of debating and deciding important issues in their communities: it offers "a lingering paradigm of an alternative mode of participatory self-government, a nucleus around which analogous modes might grow."[8] By allowing people to become engaged with and responsible for the Constitution and its application, people would begin to make it their own and perhaps be more willing to take its requirements seriously.

Working Constitutional Juries

As with any idea or proposal, the proof of the pudding will be in the eating. Consequently, it will be important to recommend the kind of arrangements that might be put in place to ensure that constitutional juries will be able to fulfil their democratic potential and possibilities. Attention will need to be paid to a number of critical objections that might be made to such an innovative and radical proposal – how large should juries be, how will the membership of constitutional juries be determined, what qualifications or training prospective members might be expected to have, how long will jury service last, how will those cases for jury review be selected, what will be the effect of any decisions made, and the like. Any final or detailed choice about such matters will, of course, be the prerogative of the people themselves, perhaps as decided by the periodic constitutional conventions.[9] Nevertheless, mindful that both the devil and the angel are in the details, some suggestions can be made about the pros and cons of particular alternatives and approaches.

In deciding upon the optimal size of a constitutional jury, a balance will need to be made between two competing imperatives – to increase the number of people involved and to ensure the efficacy of its work. There is no easy or obvious method by which to resolve this tension. However, there is little reason to imagine that constitutional juries must be restricted to the present-day size of Supreme Courts; they tend to have a membership between nine and sixteen. However, although they sit in smaller benches, some courts have a much greater pool of eligible judges to choose from;

France has about 120 and Spain has over seventy. Across their histories, the Supreme Courts of Canada and the United States have grown from six to nine judges. The initial increases were based upon a rising population base. If that notion was used today (when the populations of both countries have increased more than tenfold from their beginnings), the membership of the courts would now be closer to ninety. While those numbers may seem large and unruly, there are many reasons to press for an increase in the size of the Supreme Courts – they would be more representative of the population; they would likely be more diverse in make-up; they could hear more cases, especially if divided into several benches; less power would go to so-called swing votes; and a broader range of political views could be canvassed and expressed.[10]

If this is true for judicial bodies, then the argument for increased membership of constitutional juries is even more pressing and persuasive. Because these second-look bodies are as much like legislatures as courts (in that they are popularly chosen and openly political), the size of constitutional juries might well exceed ninety. The membership of the Canadian and American legislatures is much higher than the courts: the two-house American Congress has 535 members and the two-house Canadian Parliament has 443 members. Also, an argument can be made that the size of these bodies should be even higher if they are to keep better pace with population growth. Nonetheless, it suffices to say that the membership of constitutional juries could easily be much the same as that of current legislatures in relative size and representativeness. Such a figure would keep the level of popular participation relatively high and still be manageable for the purposes of debate and decision-making. There will be no need to have only one constitutional jury at work at one time; democracy can be well served by multiple second-look chambers in place.

The selection of citizens for membership on constitutional juries could be achieved in a number of ways. An obvious method would be to follow a similar electoral path to that recommended for legislatures.[11] While this has much to recommend it, a better and more democratic way would perhaps be to determine membership by lot (sortition), especially if membership was to be for limited terms. This is the way juries are selected today; an eligible pool is selected and then selection is done randomly. Although not at all part of the contemporary political process or mindset, selection by lot offers a number of benefits – all people have an equal chance of selection; there is a better chance of diverse representation; it extends the range of popular participation; and there is less likelihood of factionalism developing. For example, in Ancient Greece, juries of 501 citizens were empowered to decide all governance issues. Although the pool of candidates there was much smaller and much more elite (i.e., no women, slaves, propertyless), this can easily be corrected; pool eligibility for jury membership would be determined by the same criteria in use for general elections. Once citizens have sat on juries, they will no longer be eligible for future membership; this will both allow people to get on with their personal lives and guard against the dubious development of an expert class of jurypersons.

Of course, some will contend that reliance on such a serendipitous process trivializes and even denigrates the overall political process; it almost ensures that the "best and brightest" will be overlooked. But this is a possible strength from a strongly democratic standpoint in light of the experience with judicial review; the best and the brightest tend to become its own elite and develop a narrow and often self-serving political outlook disconnected from the population at large. This scepticism towards the capacity of ordinary individuals to assume such responsibility and exercise judgment in a considered manner, after vigourous debate and an exchange of competing views, lies at the root of a discredited constitutionalism. As with their legislative colleagues, jurypersons will be able to enlist a range of resources to help them fulfil their duties; this might include some initial education in constitutional history and tradition. Also, citizens would be able to forego or defer participation as best suits their own lives and other commitments. As a corollary of this, it will be important that people are able to fulfil their civic responsibilities without fear of losing employment or other advantages. Also, these constitutional jurypersons will be expected to maintain a standard of independence that is appropriate to their role and responsibilities: they must not only act in good faith but also avoid conflicts of interest and improper influences (e.g., financial incentives, self-dealing).

Also, these constitutional juries can be organized along local lines, although the initial application of their decisions could have national effect. There might well be a national constitutional jury that would be able to determine which local decisions might be reconsidered. However, such a body would need to cultivate an approach that did not facilitate a slide into the familiar situation of hierarchical supremacy that is presently an entrenched and problematic feature of courts as the guardians of constitutional meaning and application. Importantly, there will be no need to take a legalistic stance towards the bindingness of earlier precedents; the doctrine of *stare decisis* would no longer apply. Jurypersons will be aware of what other juries have determined and will be free to use that knowledge how they best see fit, but they will be under no obligation either to follow earlier decisions for the sake of it nor ignore them arbitrarily. Because jury debate and any resulting decision will be openly political in nature, the context and shifting focus of popular values will be more easily calibrated and handled.

A different or additional option might be to give the national or local legislative body the power to override the decisions of constitutional juries in exceptional circumstances. This kind of legislative process would not be dissimilar to the section 33 "notwithstanding provisions" of the Canadian Charter.[12] However, mindful that a legislature would have originally enacted the disputed and now unconstitutional legislation, it would be preferable to require any use of such an override to be approved by a special majority of around two-thirds of legislators. In this way, the competing pushes and pulls of democratic participation and representative decision-making might be more adequately balanced and implemented across a range of institutions; the democratic constitution would remain both flexible and stable. Finally, a constitutional jury would have the option, if the issue was sufficiently important and controversial, to trigger the calling of a periodic constitutional convention to consider a new drafting of a particular provision in the constitution rather than merely an override of a particular piece of disputed legislation.

Conclusion

Once courts are thought of as being part of government and judges, therefore, as being bureaucrats (rather than as a separate institution and non-governmental actors), then the option of transforming adjudicatory bodies into representative and non-professional juries becomes more understandable. As part of the general governmental apparatus, the democratic status of constitutional juries will be better attained and assured. When it is grasped that constitutional juries have no need to strive to be non-political, the requirement for them to be primarily democratic in membership and operation also becomes more apparent. Indeed, it is not that constitutionalism will be weaker under such an arrangement, but that it will actually be stronger because it will have become an aspect of strong democracy, not a check or challenge to it. In this way, the constitution will advance the interests of democracy because it will be an integral part of that democracy in both power and prestige. The replacement of courts by juries will facilitate this achievement.

chapter ten

A Time for Change:
Democratic Constitutions

The critique of the constitutionalist stance from a strongly democratic perspective, of course, is not an end in itself. The whole thrust of such an assault is to clear the ground and begin the task of constructing a set of constitutional arrangements that better advance the democratic project – to give people the opportunity and responsibility to participate directly and regularly in their own governance. In completing such a task, the critic is in something of a bind – they must be imbued with the spirit of democratic emancipation but resist the temptation to determine what practical arrangements and processes best embody and effect that political ambition. To put it more pointedly, the democrat must not dictate the cut and shape of a society's constitutional set-up and thereby usurp the very notion and practice of self-rule that a strong democracy demands and insists upon. To do otherwise, no matter how genuine the critics' democratic credentials or how well-intentioned their insights, is to slide back into the elitist, fundamentalist, and too "angelic" mindset of the discredited constitutionalists. As Mahatma Ghandi cautioned, "Whatever you do for me but without me, you do to me." Instead, the challenge and burden of the democrat is to open up an institutional space and propose transformative measures so that people can create and shape (as well as, importantly, re-create and re-shape) their own constitutional context. There is no precise blueprint, therefore, that democracy can or should follow.

In line with this imperative, this chapter offers a series of proposals for how it might be possible to become more democratic in organizing the constitutional scheme of government. The first part consolidates the failings of the constitutionalist approach as a prelude to mapping a better path forward to a more democratic scheme of governance; there is no one fixed or final destination to be reached, only a series of democratic paths to be followed. In the second part, I recommend the establishment of a constitutional convention as a forum for designing and drafting the constitution. The third part explores some of the tasks that such a convention would need to tackle in fulfilling its allotted responsibilities as a democratic forum. In the final part, I look at possible ways to amend or obviate the constitution outside of constitutional conventions. Throughout the chapter, the guiding caution is that to be pro-constitution is not in itself to be anti-democratic: the challenge is to ensure that any constitutional checks on democracy are made in the name and cause of democracy, not some other set of constitutionalist values and political ambitions.

The Democratic Challenge

A good place to begin this challenge is to take stock of the democratic failings of the existing ideas and practices of constitutionalism. By doing this, it will be possible, at least, to mark off those areas and commitments that any democratic replacement must avoid and, in the process, rectify. Moreover, this stocktaking will help to focus any different approach or deviation and enable it to deliver better on the promise of a thoroughly democratic style and structure of democratic governance. Importantly, any proposals for future change must begin from where we are and ensure that it is a democratic sensibility and dynamic that drives us to where we would like to be. Achieving democracy by undemocratic means is a betrayal of the democracy ideal itself. This drive towards a stronger democracy is an exciting and fraught task; it involves some devilish laughter and a refusal to forget.

There are several difficulties that strong constitutionalism has created and embedded in the current system of political governance. Indeed, almost all of their bedrock commitments have been shown to be both unworkable and unattainable. In an important sense, these precepts are more honoured in their breach than in their observance:

- *Democracy is the jewel in the constitutional crown* – Although much lip service is paid to the justificatory centrality of democracy in the constitutionalists' scheme of governance, there is little follow-through on this. From its earliest beginnings, there is a persistent and sizeable gap between the constitutional theory and the historical practice. Indeed, a crucial and foundational feature of constitutionalism for both jurists and judges is that constitutions do contain and constrict the reach and effect of democratic politics;
- *Constitutions act as a check on elite control* – The constitutionalist mindset is so focused on the fear of democratic majoritarianism and popular empowerment that it overlooks the stranglehold that elite groups have on the political process. Indeed, a perverse effect of this public-centred approach is that it actually works to shield such elite private power from popular scrutiny and tends to imbue it with political legitimacy. This is nowhere more true than in the privileging and exercise of political authority by the courts;
- *There can be a perfect constitutional arrangement* – It is a conceit of constitutionalists that such a goal is achievable in practice and/ or desirable in theory. From a strongly democratic perspective, this ambition works to sideline democratic participation by misunderstanding the nature of democratic politics as a means for popular participation. Although a constitution's longevity is defended in the name of stability and security, there can be no final balancing between the demands of constitutionalism and pushes of democracy;
- *There is a lasting constitution* – It is a pretence of constitutionalists that the constitution remains almost fixed and unchanged over its lifespan unless and until it is formally amended. The reality is that the constitution is constantly changing through informal methods of alteration. Whether by shifting conventions or mostly by judicial reinterpretations, the overall constitutional scheme undergoes continuing rejigging through the actions and decisions of elite governmental agencies – change is the name of the constitutional game;

- *A constitution is a higher form of law* – This idea reinforces and elevates the constitutionalist claim that constitutions are above partisan politics and superior to ordinary laws that result from the regular political process. It suggests that some values are so universal, uncontestable, and of a transcendent order that they can and should be insulated from political intervention and generational change. As suspect as this assumption is, it motivates the defence that such constitutions need to be protected from political and democratic interference;

- *Constitutions are confined to control of public power* – This notion perpetuates the false belief that the state is the major threat to people's freedom, personhood, and quality of life. Although it is absolutely important to check the uses and abuses of state power, it is also vital to curb the excesses of private and elite power. Moreover, the exclusive focus on public power enables private power to be exercised with an undeserved degree of political legitimacy and scrutiny;

- *Constitutions are neutral frameworks within which diverse politics can thrive* – This pretence has considerable ideological effect. Constitutions have been not only hijacked by one side or another at different times but also passed off as being somehow neutral and non-ideological in substance and effect. In practice, the constitution becomes one more site for political contestation as competing ideological tendencies vie for popular support and constitutional dominance;

- *Courts are neutral and unaligned agencies of governance* – Although the claim of neutrality is a condition for the success of the constitutionalist project, judges are unable to fulfil their constitutional responsibilities without resorting to a range of contested and ideological issues. This is particularly apparent when the historical arc of changing legal doctrine is examined and understood. Despite the valiant efforts of some democratically inspired jurists, there is no theory that can save judges from their own political nature.

Taken together, these form a powerful bill of indictment against the constitutionalist project. When viewed from a strongly democratic standpoint, that project is found to be severely wanting; the occasional and much-hyped trappings of democracy serve to hide an elitist practice of governance that falls well short of its own standards of justification and success, let alone any democratic ones. Of course, the historical fact that societies like the United States and Canada, which are in thrall to a constitutionalist approach, have made significant contributions to an improvement in its citizens' lives both in terms of material benefits and just outcomes cannot be ignored or trivialized. However, a complacent and even smug attribution of those gains to constitutionalism is to be resisted. The democrat insists that these advances have not come without considerable cost, have not been as uniformly or especially successful as their proponents claim, have not been achieved very quickly, and, most importantly, have been achieved in spite of rather than because of the enduring attachment to constitutionalism. Whatever specific attainments can be credited to the constitutionalist approach, there are better and more compelling ways to put society on a more just and more emancipatory footing – a vigorous and robust embrace of a thoroughly democratic practice of politics.

Accordingly, the time is ripe to abandon the constitutionalist mindset and its derivative institutional arrangements and informing routines. Instead, the onus is on democrats to present a more compelling vision of democracy's possibilities by tracing out the general contours of such a democratic commitment and its institutional implications and entailments. As I have been at pains to emphasize, this is not only not an easy task but also one that democratic theorists must approach with caution and humility; they must practice what they preach. There is no mandate or excuse for anyone imposing their preference or recommendations on others, no matter how appealing or good-hearted. Democracy is about people making their own choices for themselves. This means that democrats (including and perhaps especially critics like me) must restrain themselves from being hubristic or patronizing; people, like commentators, must be allowed to make their own choices, even if they appear to others to be mistaken.

However, there still remains a role for democratic theorists. With a suitable modesty of purpose and design, they must strive to propose, not decree; they must persuade, not pontificate; and they must recommend, not validate. With that in mind, I turn to offer the outline of one possible democratic account of constitutional politics. The hope is that a reliance on the "the five basic precepts of democratic advancement" can help bridge the existing divide between democracy's past and future, between its commitment and achievement, and between its vision and reality.[1] In particular, these guidelines can better inform and energize the project of democratic renewal in the constitutional context. Of course, the precise scope of the various aspects of constitutional governance – amendment procedures, constitutional content, scope of rights, composition of review body, and so on – will be for the people themselves to determine and re-determine as and when they see fit. This is a massive and demanding responsibility, but it is also a wonderfully invigorating opportunity to put democratic participation front and centre in the political affairs of society.

Constitutional Forums

If a constitution is to have any chance of meeting the exacting demands of strong democracy, it must at least be nurtured and drafted in strongly democratic settings and circumstances. Unlike the originating circumstances of the American and Canadian Constitutions, people must play an almost exclusive and decisive role. While all the people cannot be fully part of the process all of the time, it is essential that people do have control and substantial input into not only the content of the constitution but also the terms and conditions that shape debate and decision-making. This, of course, will be no small feat. Among other things, it demands a constant check upon both the general design and the practical details of the democratic processes of constitution-making. Without a strongly democratic beginning and foundation, the resulting constitution will be destined to fail as a democratic achievement. Moreover, because there is no fixed or final way of achieving this democratic state of affairs, there will need to be flexibility as well as foresight in making the kind of political compromises that will be required.

One way to start would be through a "constitutional election." A generalized proposal for a new constitution might be debated and settled upon by the people's elected representatives and then put to a popular vote. Although this has some attraction, it would ultimately fail the demanding standards of strong democracy. First, elections have become less a measure for the expression of popular opinion and more an exercise in elitist manipulation.[2] This is made all the more problematic when, since finance has been allowed to corrupt franchise, a faux populism has reasserted itself and given rise to a more divisive and frankly crypto-elitist politics. Second (and most importantly), the crucial democratic dimension of public debate and popular engagement in formulating the contents of the proposed constitution would be foregone; the elite would even more directly be able to shape and control the initial and important phase of the constitution-making process. Instead, strong democracy asks that people take upon themselves this educative and bedrock responsibility. While this will not do away entirely with elitist manipulation, it will push towards a more genuinely democratic process that will be more extensive, more equal, more involved, and more transparent in its participation than less so.

What might such a process look like? Mindful that the democratic best ought not to be the enemy of the democratic better and that it is for the people themselves to determine how their opinions and voices can be best expressed and incorporated, the notion of a "constitutional forum" has much to recommend itself. This would be a body that is convened with the express purpose of designing and drafting the constitution; it would have the unfettered power and responsibility to fulfil its mandate. Its membership might be between around 350 and 400; any fewer would fail to ensure that a diverse range of interests would be represented and any more would hamper the group's capacity to debate and reach conclusions that would garner sufficient overall support. The procedures that the forum will adopt and operate with would be the first item of business for the members. Also, once chosen, the members would have a sufficient budget to ensure that they could access whatever resources (e.g., staff, data, advisers) that they thought would be necessary to complete the job properly. Further, the members would be paid a reasonable and fair salary for their exertions; their existing employment and economic situation would be protected during the fulfilment of their democratic duties.

Of course, the identity of the members who comprise the forum and how they would be chosen is crucial to its democratic legitimacy. It should be a given that the members as a group would need to reflect the overall diversity among the general population (i.e., race, gender, class, age). The more difficult issue would be how these delegates would be chosen from among the entire citizenry. The basic choices are those of random selection, meritocratic qualification, and democratic selection. The first two, as stand-alone options, seem to fail the exacting standards of democratic governance. Whereas random choice has its attractions (in particular, that it will not result in elite interests or members being overrepresented), it does not reinforce the central idea of strong democracy that people must have a direct and continuing involvement in decisions made on their behalf. On the other hand, meritocratic qualification too easily collapses into the constitutionalist status quo in which so-called experts hijack the process and impose their own self-interested values under the guise of wisdom and objectivity; this is the very problem that democracy is supposed to resolve, not facilitate.

The only viable, if decidedly second-best solution is to go with democratic selection. In any modern society, like the United States or Canada, that has vast numbers of citizens, encompasses competing cultures and traditions, and covers large geographic territories, there will need to be some mode of voting. It goes almost without saying that such voting must be done in accordance with the most demanding and scrupulous norms of strong democracy. So, in order to avoid the tribalism of political party elections, citizens can be asked to volunteer for temporary office. Equal public funding (with no external or private funding) would be available to all candidates who make their way on to the ballot. Voting can be done in localized constituencies that will be as free as possible from the ills of gerrymandering; this will avoid the dubious appeal of a first-past-the-post system. The elected members will have their full-time jobs protected and be paid a reasonable salary for the period of their membership. The forum would be entrusted to set their own schedule and timeline. However, members will know that timeliness is an important democratic virtue and will be a spur to their deliberations and decisions.

From a democratic perspective, an important consideration is the role that these elected members of the constitutional forum will assume. Again, this will largely depend on the views of the members themselves, but there is a participatory tendency towards the idea that representative members will see themselves as something between a delegate and a trustee. The more common stance is that of delegates who are authorized to act on behalf of those who elected them; they are not empowered to do more than speak for the interests of the local electorate. In contrast, trustees are given licence to deliberate and act in line with their own understanding of what is in the public interest generally.[3] While they cannot ignore or oppose the interests of their constituents, they are not entirely beholden to them. One way to think about it is that trustees are more than crude mouthpieces for others; they can add their own accent and content to the discursive and political voices of those constituents. Accordingly, they would ultimately be accountable and answerable to the group that they represent, but they have a wider allegiance to the community as a whole. Strong democracy is advanced by the recognition that politics is not only quantitative (i.e., counting and aggregating people's preferences) but also qualitative (i.e., adding a critical and responsive element to that process); the exchange of ideas in political debate is an indispensable feature of a vibrant and mature democracy.

This idea and practice of a constitutional forum draws upon, but is not limited to the example of the American founding convention of the summer of 1787. In many ways, that almost four-month-long event contains the best and worst of democratic possibility. At the end of the eighteenth century, the franchise was so limited that it is impossible to view that gathering as even barely representative, let alone strongly democratic in origins and ambition: it was a thoroughly elite occasion whose membership was drawn from a very narrow strata of society (i.e., male, white, land-owning, unenslaved) and whose mandate was only tangentially democratic in spirit or achievement. Indeed, most people were excluded from playing any part at all. James Madison's view – "the public voice, pronounced by the representatives of the people, will be more consonant to the public good than if pronounced by the people themselves"[4] – accurately summed it up. The best that might be said of this state of affairs is that it was only democratic insofar as the assumed understanding of what counted as democratic at that time was so rudimentary as to be undeserving of what can now fairly be credited as democratic today. Although there was engaged debate and a sense of purpose and compromise, this did not achieve the kind of mythic nation-making of historical legend that is still often recorded; partisan politics was always in play and never far below the surface.[5]

To be clear, this is no bad thing. A democratic sensibility is practical and realistic. It eschews the trappings of politics as an almost mystical art form; it recognizes that politics is not something to be avoided or transcended but to be met head on. The democratic forum that I am suggesting must not be thought as having the opportunity or responsibility to generate a constitution that is somehow fixed and final. It should not consider itself to be a major part of the myth-making machinery of a partial political dynasty. This kind of thinking and effort is anathema to a strongly democratic sensibility. While members of the forum will strive to settle upon a constitution that does more than advance and instantiate people's immediate and perhaps ephemeral interests, they will not arrogate to themselves another-worldly role of stipulating the values and visions of future generations; they will work that important space between topicality and transcendence. In striving to toe this line, the words of an aging Thomas Jefferson are to the point:

> Some men look at constitutions with sanctimonious reverence, and deem them like the arc of the covenant, too sacred to be touched. They ascribe to the men of the preceding age a wisdom more than human, and suppose what they did to be beyond amendment ... But I know also, that laws and institutions must go hand in hand with the progress of the human mind. As that becomes more developed, more enlightened,

as new discoveries are made, new truths disclosed, and manners and
opinions change with the change of circumstances, institutions must
advance also, and keep pace with the times.[6]

It is with this spirit of humility and awareness that the members of
such a constitutional forum should approach their task. They must
resist the temptation to imagine that they are godly or superhuman.
In order to encourage that and guard against unwelcome hubris, the
constitution should have a lifespan of twenty-five years at most.[7]
After that period of time, the existing constitution should become
defunct and a new constitutional forum called. This measure would
not only ensure that each new generation would be entitled to determine the constitutional terms of their own politics but it would also
impress on the members of a constitutional forum that they were not
encumbered by the unhelpful ambition of setting the terms and conditions for generations to come. Theirs would be an effort to do the
best that they could in light of prevailing circumstances and possibilities. Of course, it might be that later forums would continue and
affirm the efforts of earlier forums. But, as Oliver Wendell Holmes Jr.
observed, "historic continuity with the past is not a duty, it is only a
necessity."[8] In this way, strong democracy would not only be exemplified but also be protected: a constitution would become an institutional device that was in the service of democracy, not a democracy
that was in servitude to a constitution.

Finally, a looming challenge for democrats is how to harness the
potential of technology for advancing and broadening the democratic project. Contrary to the mythology of much extant theorizing,
democracy is not something that can only function in the cozy (and
elitist) confines of yesterday's founding generations. As the reach of
the internet and online discourse expands, there is much to learn from
digitalization generally and from blockchain platforms particularly;
they offer exciting ways to streamline and deepen the opportunities
for more people being able to play a more regular and extensive participatory role in governance and policy formation. However, along
with these possible gains, there also comes some serious threats to the
inclusive dimension of democracy and its anti-elitist thrust. The fear
is that democracy will fall victim to a tendency towards entrenching

a technocratic elite in which the more technologically sophisticated (and richer) segments of society will squeeze out and gain greater power than the technologically unsophisticated (and poorer) ones. All of this recommends that technology can neither be entirely rejected nor fully embraced in a modern democratic state. As is often the case, the challenge is to utilize new technological resources and openings in such a way that public debate is more likely to be extended and enhanced, not confined and debased.[9]

Constitutional Content

Once a constitutional convention is convened, its membership settled, and its internal procedures decided upon, it will be incumbent upon the group to determine the content and scope of the constitution. Strong democracy recommends that there will be no formal constraints or restrictions upon what they can and cannot include. In line with a truly democratic dynamic, any compromises made will be required to show that they are intended to advance popular participation, not limit it. As such, any checks and balances or trade-offs introduced will be done not with democracy but within it. Also, the convention members will recognize that, in mapping out the general distribution of power across governmental entities and agencies, there will need to be a balance between generality and specificity; the constitution must provide a clear but not detailed account of who will exercise power, how it will be exercised, and what the procedures for accountability are. At bottom, the democratically appointed and democratically legitimated convention will be left to its own devices in promoting and protecting democracy.

One of the more taxing issues on the constitutional convention's agenda will be to decide what to do about the establishment, enumeration, and protection of rights. As a general notion, there is no necessary antithesis between the existence of a rights-based constitution and a commitment to strong democracy. Indeed, it can be cogently argued that the two are mutually reinforcing. However, the convention should reject the basic and rejected constitutionalist claim that constitutional rights are somehow the stuff of higher and more transcendent commitments and should be treated accordingly. Instead, the convention will adopt a more pragmatic and realistic approach. It should view individual's and group's entitlements against the abuse of power to be paramount and central to the democratic project, but better protected through their recognition as being the product of contingent political agreement with no higher or other-worldly definition or validation.

In building upon that appreciation, the convention will have to make the critical decision about whether a regime of freedoms and entitlements is better promoted by a special mention and listing in the constitution or better left to the workings of the regular democratic and legislative process. For traditional constitutionalists, this will be condemned as a false or easy choice – a designation and enumeration of individual rights is a constitutional must. However, this is by no means obvious from a strongly democratic standpoint. For instance, Jeremy Waldron has insisted that, as a historical matter and within a working democracy, rights will be at least as well protected as they would be through existing practices of judicial review: "ordinary legislative procedures can [protect rights] … and an additional layer of final review by courts adds little to the process except a rather insulting form of disenfranchisement and a legalistic obfuscation of the moral issues at stake in our disagreements about rights."[10] This is a bold claim, but one that receives considerable historical support, particularly in regard to social entitlement (e.g., health care, welfare benefits, and housing). By leaving such matters to the legislative branch of government, there is the added advantage that people will appreciate better that rights are not an elite act of the *noblesse oblige*, but are part and parcel of people's mundane political engagements. It will be for the convention to make that kind of contingent and strategic calculation as it comes to debate and finalize its work.

If the conventional members do decide to incorporate a charter of rights within the constitution, there are a number of vital issues that they will have to confront and resolve. These include:

- *Who are to be the recipients of such rights?* – Although this may seem obvious, there are several possibilities – citizens, individuals, visitors, organizations, animals, and the like. The history of constitutional law reveals that this initial decision has resulted in some fundamental conflicts, especially around the recognition of corporate entities and its consequences;

• *What particular group of rights are to be recognized and enforced?* – This is also a matter of contested political judgment. Decisions will need to be made about whether only civil and personal rights (e.g., communication, religious belief, and criminal) are incorporated or whether socio-economic and collective rights (e.g., shelter, jobs, and collective bargaining) are also to be included;

• *What is the scope and nature of each particular right to be?* – Without expecting a detailed and comprehensive listing, it will be significant to determine whether all rights are to be extended to all right-holders equally (e.g., citizens, visitors, and aliens) and what the content of the more general rights entail (e.g., communication/ pornography, criminal/voting, and religious belief/activities);

• *How to resolve a clash of competing rights?* – A range of rights (e.g., communication, equality, and assembly) do not operate in isolation or independence from each other; they interact and potentially intrude upon each other. Resolving that tension between, for example, religious liberty and racial or sexual equality is a very difficult challenge that will need to be addressed, at least in general terms;

• *Against whom can each right be exercised?* – There is no neutral or definitive explanation of when particular rights are in play and who is required to respect such rights. Abuses of power come in many forms and from many sources (e.g., governmental, corporate, private individuals, and universities), so it will be imperative to indicate in what circumstances particular rights can be respected and enforced; and

• *How is the public interest to be balanced against an individual's claim?* – It seems generally clear that, even if some rights are considered fundamental (e.g., communication, voting, equality), they are not absolute in their application and must on occasion bend to the broader public interest (war, communication, and national security). Again, suggesting how some kind of striking balance might be achieved would be helpful.

A constitutional convention might decide that the fulfilment of these tasks is so difficult and so context-specific that the creation of a specially designated tribunal, like a constitutional jury, is demanded. This possibility is not inherently anti-democratic or elitist. Everything will depend on the nature of that institution, its membership, and its democratic legitimacy. As should be obvious, the reliance on a second-look institution to put some flesh on the constitutional skeleton and to resolve discrete disputes should not necessarily lead to the reintroduction of judicial review as it exists today. Indeed, it is essential that such a move is entirely resisted; courts as constitutional arbiters have no place in a community committed to strong democracy. Instead, considerable attention will need to be given to the role, range, and responsibilities of such an agency.[11] Provided that it respects and meets the participatory standards of strong democracy, such a body can enhance, not undermine the dynamic achievements of a democratic mode of governance.

Finally, there is the tricky matter of whether the completed constitution decided on by the convention should be submitted for overall ratification by the general electorate. The initial instinct is to require this on the basis that more direct participation is always better than less. However, there is also the problem of ensuring that democracy does not start to collapse under its own institutional and operative weight; too much talking and not enough doing is likely to sap a community's political will. Nevertheless, in this case (and mindful that such a constitutional convention would only occur once every twenty-five years), the preferable response is to proceed with a society-wide ratifying vote. If that referral to the overall citizenry is unsuccessful, then the convention would have to reconvene (perhaps with newly elected members), recanvass social views, and begin its work again. This is far from being a desirable state of affairs but a necessary one if both the constitution's authority and the democracy's legitimacy is to be maintained.

Constitutional Amendment

It seems apparent that it should be possible to amend a constitution as changing circumstances and democratic choices develop. This is in stark contrast to the current situation in which the possibilities for change are so remote as to make the existing constitutions impermeable to formal change except in marginal and unimportant matters. Of course, constitutional law does change through the informal, but no less effective interventions of the courts and government actors. However, reliance upon the unelected, unrepresentative, and unaccountable work of judges fits very poorly, if at all, with a democratic imperative. The constitutionalist defence of judicial review is unpersuasive and anti-democratic.[12] In a strong democracy, if there are to be changes to the constitution, they must be achieved and understood in a thoroughly democratic way; institutional transparency as well as popular participation are indispensable to democratic legitimacy.

Nevertheless, it seems reasonable, as constitutionalists argue, that changes to the constitution should be regarded as a little out of the normal course of politics and not part of the run-of-the-mill kind of legislative change. This does not mean that change should be beyond the practical reach of regular democratic bodies, but that constitutional change should demand a slightly more exacting and openly democratic process than other changes. Mindful that a constitutional convention must take place every twenty-five years, the chance that the constitution will become so entrenched as to be beyond popular correction would no longer be as serious a possibility. That being said, it is important that the constitution should be amenable to change in line with democratic wishes if unexpected and unwanted situations and outcomes arise. The fact that a second-look and on-the-ground constitutional tribunal might arrive at decisions that run counter to broader democratic sensibilities and opinions will mean that some mode of interim constitutional amendment should be available.

The immediate candidate for such a role would be a similarly organized and elected constitutional convention that is envisaged to occur every generation. However, this is a cumbersome process and, while sustainable for a complete review of the constitution, seems to be unsuited to the more piecemeal task at hand. The special and specific amendment of the constitution is an occasion that must bear a strongly democratic imprint, but the process must not become so elaborate and onerous that it will impose more burdens than benefits. Accordingly, I maintain that the amendment process might be performed by the legislative branch itself, but under slightly more exacting standards than for ordinary legislative enactments. This is when the current "notwithstanding clause" of the Canadian Constitution, suitably adjusted, might strike an attractive balance between democratic empowerment and institutional efficiency.

It will be remembered that section 33 of the Canadian Constitution allows the federal Parliament or a provincial legislature to declare that an act "shall operate notwithstanding a provision included in s. 2 or ss. 7–15" of the Charter of Rights (i.e., all the basic rights except voting). While its exercise only works within the legislative area over which the federal or provincial government has jurisdiction and lasts for five years, a simple majority in Parliament or a provincial legislative assembly is all that is needed to effect such a significant constitutional veto. Of course, the provision does result in an amendment to the Constitution going forward. To date, although the inclusion of this provision was an essential component of the initial constitutional deal, its existence has been treated as aberrational, and use of it is often condemned as being offensive not only to Canada's constitutional tradition but also to its democratic commitments.[13] This is simply an overwrought response that is inspired by a constitutionalist mindset writ large; it puts the constitutional cart well before or even beyond the democratic horse.

Understood from a strongly democratic perspective, such a constitutional overrule might be utilized to handle constitutional amendments. Two additions or alterations might be appropriate to make this more palatable as a democratic mode of formal amendment. First, a simple majority might remain sufficient if a legislature only wanted to exempt specific legislation from the constitution's application. Also, a new extension of that exemption would be demanded after every democratic election. Secondly, if a formal constitutional amendment was intended, a stiffer, but not unreachable special two-thirds majority might be required. This compromise might assuage some of the constitutionalist concerns as well as satisfy strong democrats who insist upon the primacy of democratic rule over constitutional authority. Future legislatures would be empowered to introduce their own amendments. Further, a full constitutional convention would remain on a fixed twenty-five-year schedule; this would ensure that a strong and full democratic process would be activated. In this way, the balance between stability and flexibility might be achieved in a way that ensured that citizens had the ultimate say in constitutional as well as governmental matters.

Conclusion

There is nothing definitive or final about the proposals that I have made. They are intended as possible strategies to be adopted by citizens and their governmental institutions as they seek to organize (and reorganize) themselves in line with a strongly democratic dynamic. As Larry Kramer puts it, "The choice is not between order and chaos or stability and anarchy, but between different types of stability and different mechanisms for achieving it."[14] In striking a balance between stability and change I have kept firmly in mind the basic insistence that, if limits are to be placed on regular and real participation, it can only be in the service of democracy itself and not some other goal or value. To do otherwise would be to betray the democratic project and to succumb to the empty blandishments of discredited constitutionalism. Constitutionalism must be understood, not as constitutionalists do, as being not in competition with democracy but as an integral and component part of democracy. As such, I have tried to keep faith with the rejoinder that American President Woodrow Wilson made to his critics, "The cure for the ills of democracy is more, not less democracy."

chapter eleven

Laughing and Remembering: Putting Democracy First

As much as Alexis de Tocqueville sang the praises of democracy's possibilities in nineteenth-century America, he was also acutely aware of its future challenges and historical failings. Indeed, what he celebrated as the virtues of democracy were balanced against the vices of its vulnerability to a new aristocratic threat. This ambivalence was captured by the tension between the opposing views of early nineteenth-century political rivals, John Adams and Thomas Jefferson; they died fortuitously within hours of each other on 4 July 1826, on the fiftieth anniversary of the Declaration of Independence. One of their most relevant disagreements was over whether American society would develop along broadly egalitarian lines as Jefferson hoped (notwithstanding his own racist views and practices) or whether it would breed its own wealth-based aristocracy as Adams feared (notwithstanding his own privileged place in society). As a result, a Jefferson-influenced view saw no real need for a strong central government to discipline markets and interfere in the natural order of things, whereas an Adams-inflected view maintained that a strong national government was essential in order to regulate rampant capitalism's oligarchic tendencies and to promote democracy's egalitarian aspirations.[1]

In this regard, this book has taken sides with John Adams's views, though not his status – it is very much driven by the belief that a democratic mode of governance is the most significant and productive ideal around which to achieve and organize an egalitarian and progressive society. A commitment to strong democracy and a weak constitutionalism is the best combination. As exemplified by the constitutionalist approach that I have explained and criticized, democracy has always been put in the service of some other political ideal and thereby constrained in the name of it. My effort has been to identify that dynamic and to rebalance it in favour of a more liberating commitment to strong democracy. While there are and can be no guarantees about the success of a steadfast commitment to strong democracy, any compromises with it should be made in order to advance democracy, not constrict it.

Closings and Openings

Some contemporary critics, however, have not been as balanced or as cautious in their appraisals of liberal democracy as Tocqueville. Most notably, in the early 1990s, Francis Fukuyama offered a paean to American democracy, at least in its late twentieth-century liberal incarnation. He waxes optimistically about "the end of history" and its arrival at its final destination in the reassuring province of today's liberal democracy: "The end point of mankind's ideological evolution [was] the universalization of Western liberal democracy as the final form of human government."[2] This is heady stuff. Of course, from a global perspective, this final assessment has proved to be both premature and entirely optimistic; the rise of right-wing populism has proven a considerable fly in the liberal ointment. But, even when Fukuyama first made his provocative prognostication in 1989, it was also highly contestable as a matter of both history and philosophy. For all the real gains made by liberalism, there was and continues to be the running-up of a considerable democratic deficit that undermined the anti-elitist ambitions and practices of a genuine democratic sensibility. Much of this democratic backsliding can be attributed to North American society's preoccupation with liberal ideas and governmental practices; elitism has gone from strength to strength.

The contemporary crisis of liberal democracy and the rise of a populist backlash combine to create a troubling state of affairs. It has operated to close down democratic politics in the name of a hegemonic and negative view of what democracy is and what it could be. But, at the risk of being too much of a Pollyanna, I also maintain that it represents an opportunity to reconstruct politics and governance in line with a stronger commitment to democracy. We are well past simply striving to fulfil the promise of representative democracy as understood within the liberal democratic canon; this can too easily turn into a partial and face-saving exercise in a faux democracy that fails to root out all forms of elitism.[3] The fracturing of the liberal establishment has led in the short term to some dark places. However, like much else, it might also be a phase that can be used to democratic advantage; there may be democratic light at the end of this political tunnel. As such, there needs to be a more concerted effort to prise the notion of "the people" from the suffocating clutches of the right-wing populists and place it within a more pluralistic, airy, and less exclusionary politics. This is a worthy and viable endeavour.

As the old saw goes, "Wherever we want to go, we will need to start that journey from where we are now." Being situated in the context of liberal democracy, it will be important to recognize that for its failings and flaws, it has much to recommend it. The challenge for democrats will be to avoid the knee-jerk response of the right-wing populists and throw the democratic baby out with the liberal bathwater. Indeed, liberal democracy has much to offer if (1) there is less of a gap between its theoretical aspirations and its lived actuality, and (2) it is deepened and broadened to address economic and class divisions that work to stifle and blunt any egalitarian and democratic thrust that it might have. Again, as Tocqueville put it, "It is not possible to conceive of [people] as eternally unequal among themselves on one point and equal on others."[4] The excesses of right-wing populism can be suitably rejected (as can the hypocrisy of many liberal democrats). Instead, the democrat can build a better polity from the ruins and rubble of liberal democracy. This will be a difficult and dangerous task, but one that is worth the effort and energy. By building it themselves, citizens will be able to shape it more closely to their own democratic purposes.

In such a transformed political culture, people might begin to appreciate that they do not need a grand theorized foundation for their commitment to democracy; they will simply need faith in themselves and the institutions that they build for themselves and for others. Most importantly, they might begin to appreciate that democratic salvation cannot be found in a commitment to a political arrangement in which there exists a constitution beyond popular reach and democratic management. Because democracy is open-ended and contestable, it has no one recipe for success, no one identity of "the people," and no one vision of the substantive good life. As such, democracy must not only accept institutionalized uncertainty but also defend and welcome it.[5] A strong democracy acknowledges that, in the same way that there is no fixed or final emancipatory project, there is no settled or fundamental scheme, especially one that is governed by elite lawyers and judges. In short, for the democrat, it is always preferable for there to be an informing dynamic of strong democracy and weak constitutionalism. The reliance on constitutional law (as opposed to democratic politics) robs people of their entitlement to be the main source of society's moral and political guidance; it saps civic energies and relegates ordinary people to also-rans. Democracy is about governance *by* the people as well as *for* and *of* the people.

Democracy First and Last

Democracies and constitutions are no laughing matter. Nor are they easily ignored or forgotten. Separately and together, they address and deal with some of the most fundamental and important issues on today's political and legal agenda. Encompassing issues as varied and vital as state power, government authority, individual liberties, citizen participation, social entitlement, and the like, these ideas go to the very heart of what it means for people to live in a just and fair society. Of course, because of this, there is a large and heated division among scholars and citizens about what democracy and constitutions entail, how they relate to each other, and why they are worth struggling over. Indeed, that division not only underlies much of the dynamics that frame and form the substance and scope of regular politics and laws but also speaks to even deeper disagreements about the nature of personal fulfilment and social engagement. As such, many think that any effort to deal with democracy and constitutions must be unfailingly serious and unremittingly earnest; there is no room for laughter or forgetfulness in such an endeavour. Obviously, I do not agree (at least when laughter is understood in the Kunderian way that I have used it).

In this book, I have taken an approach to democracy and constitutions that is about both laughter and forgetting (but hopefully not in a laughable or forgettable way). There is much to laugh about in the contemporary writing and practices of democracy and constitutions. Moreover, those activities rely upon a sustaining mode of historical amnesia and forgetting. In other words, I want to insist that laughter might be the best medicine to treat what ails the forgetful understandings and dubious practices of democracy and constitutions in the present day. Of course, this will not in itself guarantee a healthier or rude polity. But it will point to how the ills of contemporary democracy and constitutions might be cured by a more invigorated and rigorous account and practice of both democracy and constitutions. To that end, I have sought to offer an optimistic and positive project that rejects the pessimistic and negative performance of the prevailing approaches to democracy and constitutions.

Behind the controversy around the democratic legitimacy of judicial review, there lurks a much more compelling issue. The current debate tends to be polarized as a straight democratic choice between "rule by a judicial elite" or "rule by a governmental elite." As judicial review involves unelected judges invalidating the actions of elected legislators or executives, all judicial review is anti-majoritarian and, therefore, presumptively undemocratic; no theory can genuinely reconcile judicial review with majority rule. Because there is no way to bring such a project to a satisfactory conclusion, continuing attempts to do so merely exacerbate the problem of democratic legitimacy and erode the very confidence that the legal establishment is trying to maintain. As I have insisted, a better response is to acknowledge that adjudication in a society of diverse and conflicting politics is an inevitably ideological undertaking. Once this is done, courts will be seen to be necessarily antagonistic or surperfluous to democratic requirements.[6]

However, the real and neglected issue is not the judiciary's lack of democratic legitimacy or the politicization of courts, but the institutional failure of the executive and legislative branches of government to meet fully their democratic responsibilities and constitutional mandate. If governments and legislatures were more truly responsive to popular concerns and more open to popular participation, the question of what judges do would be less pressing and more incidental. Consequently, if there is a crisis in democracy, it is that it is used more as a rhetorical cloak for elitist governmental practice than as a measure and guide for popular politics; it is present-day governmental arrangements generally, not only judicial review, that fails to satisfy or even aspire to the demands of strong democracy. However, while there is no compelling argument as to why democracies should rely on judicial review, it does not follow that all power and authority should be left in the hands of omnipotent legislatures; there is absolutely no warrant to frame the debate as a zero-sum choice between legislatures and courts, as presently constituted. In short, there is a strong and "easy" case to be made for the creation of multiple possible veto points in ensuring the fulfilment of important democratic ambitions about the protection of people's rights and political entitlements. My proposal for constitutional juries flows from this understanding.

Democracy is seen to be the ultimate and first-and-last basis for legitimating government. It demands that a society have the courage of its own democratic convictions: people themselves must be trusted to decide what to do and to choose the procedures and practices through which such decisions are made over what is to be done. There is simply no rationale for deferring that task to those elites who presently hold power. As part of the governmental structure, constitutions must be designed and applied by the people, not simply on their behalf or in their name. As such, legal theorists' attention must shift towards the critical elaboration of those process-related conditions that make legal enactments and decisions more or less democratic. So informed, it will then become more apparent that outcomes and processes are not separate or separable, but are intimately connected through their democratic status and shared ambition: democratically passed laws are legitimate not because of their vague and slippery conformity with elusive "moral truths," but because they satisfy process-related democratic criteria and on the whole advance the democratic project.

There is no place for the half-hearted democrat in the truly democratic society. Although strong democrats are deeply concerned about the substantive quality of people's lives, they place more emphasis on enabling good lives than engaging in the detached search for some elusive good life. Such a preoccupation is the mark of the constitutionalist jurist. In a strong democracy, therefore, it is a point of principle and practice that the ends and means are integrated as closely as practically possible: the status and legitimacy of the initiating procedures is the benchmark against which both the legal system and any particular enactment's legitimacy can be measured. The greater the extent and quality of participation in the legislative and adjudicative process, the greater the legitimacy of their substantive pronouncements. Any other approach would betray their democratic nature and origins.

Being experimental and open as well as suspicious of any general claims to truth-validating methods, democracy is sensitive to the inevitable presence of power and its disruptive and self-serving potential. "Existing values" and "settled interests" have no democratic valence on their own. While critics and activists must work with the justificatory tools of their society, they are not condemned to work within its past decisions or remain beholden to its current orientations. The past consensus is only a starting point and the present-day accord is only a temporary respite from continuing debate and engagement. As such, extant democratic arrangements must themselves not only allow but also encourage and facilitate critical engagement. Justificatory standards endure only as long as they retain the confidence and support of the community as the best and most useful benchmarks available; they thrive and wither in a good faith debate between intelligent interlocutors about what counts as "working best."

As such, strong democracy's antipathy to elitism extends to those philosophers, sages, or experts who claim that there are some set of objective values or truths to which a democratic society must conform or by which it can be disciplined. Because they insist that there is no one set of rights entitlements or practical realization of them that will always be morally superior, strong democrats believe that it is for people themselves to determine what is best for them. Moral authority is a quality to be earned in democratic exchange, not bestowed from elsewhere; there is no independent or superior standard of moral legitimacy than that derived from the processes and procedures by which laws and legal decisions are made. In particular, there is no supra-democratic method that can be invoked or appealed to that will have greater moral authority than the society's own routine engagements through its democratic infrastructure and according to its prevailing social *ethos*. There are no conversation-ending or truth-fixing arguments about moral claims other than those that gain acceptance in engaged debate and open inquiry.

Strong democrats can make and promote enthusiastically normative arguments, but they simply cannot defend them as somehow eternal or transcendental. Moreover, for much the same reasons, strong democrats do not adopt a sceptical approach to rights; they simply maintain that there are no epistemological or political bases for rights that are above or outside the existing democratic practices that give rise to them. Political and moral rights exist and are justified to the extent that a vibrant democracy holds faith with them. This is both an exciting prospect and also a scary one for those accustomed to the constitutionalist status quo. As a result, strong democrats must be strong in their view of democracy and its possibilities, and they must be strong in maintaining and promoting their commitment to it. Democracy is not for the faint of heart or for those who think that they know what is best for others: it demands humility, not hubris and courage, not resignation. Most importantly, it asks for the present-day elite to step aside so that ordinary people can begin to control and shape their own lives and their own fates.

Laughing and Remembering

In this short book, I have tried to give voice to a form of remember-ing and laughter that encourages people not to "try to replace one type of power with another, [but] … repudiate the very principle of power and repudiate it everywhere." As such, I have claimed that this responsibility falls to democracy as the best (or "least worse," as Churchill would have it) and only available mode of political organization that can exert the necessary force against the power of elites and others. This project goes to the very core of what it means to be part of "the struggle of memory against forgetting." There is no better or more radical undertaking than this. It brings into full play the crucial and enduring relation between democracy and constitutionalism as both a debilitating historical enterprise that has promised much more than it can deliver and as a transfor-mative political practice that can become whatever people choose for it to become.

   In working towards this reclamation of memory and the aban-donment of forgetting, I have relied upon laughter as one of the unlikely devices for unlocking the potential for political eman-cipation and personal enlightenment. This book strives to adopt a devilish and laughter-filled democratic approach in the task of confronting the angelic pretensions of traditional constitutionalist thinking and its concerted effort to erase memory. As Milan Kun-dera urges, "real and total" laughter is not contrived or forced, it is "serious laughter, laughter beyond joking" that goes to the core of our being and is "without memory" – "to laugh is to live pro-foundly."[7] Strong democracy is a place that can instill that liberat-ing sense of laughing and remembering; constitutionalism is not. While not a joke, it is, like humour itself, less an escape from reality as it is from despair.

Notes

1 Democracy and Constitutions: Laughing and Forgetting

1 Gilmore, *The Ages of American Law*, 35.
2 Rawls, "The Idea of Public Reason Revisited."
3 Repplier, *Counter-Currents*, 288.
4 Kundera, *The Book of Laughter and Forgetting*, 33, 30, 257, 19, 218, 217, 218.
5 Kundera, 117, 119.
6 Kundera, 79, 81, 85–6.
7 Kundera, 81, 85–7, 100.
8 Kundera, 4, 106, 149.
9 Clymer, "Warren B. Rudman, Blunt Senator Who Led Budget Struggle, Dies at 82."

2 A Constitutionalist State of Mind: A Deeper Dive

1 Pound, "Law in Books and Law in Action."
2 McIlwain, *Constitutionalism: Ancient and Modern*, 21. See also Scruton, *A Dictionary of Political Thought*; Freidrich, *Constitutional Government and Democracy*.
3 Maddex, *Constitutions of the World*, xvi–xxii.
4 Fallon Jr., *Law and Legitimacy in the Supreme Court*, 25.
5 Elkins, Ginsburg, and Melton, *Endurance of National Constitutions*, 38.
6 Dworkin, *Is Democracy Possible Here?* 134.
7 Dworkin, 131.
8 Dworkin, 134.
9 Dworkin, 144.
10 Dworkin, 32.

11 Dworkin, 146. He also states that, democracy "cannot prescribe the procedures for testing whether the conditions for the procedures it does prescribe are met." See Dworkin, *Freedom's Law*, 33. See also Dworkin, *Justice in Robes*, 239. For more on judicial review, see page 26 in this chapter.

12 Dworkin, *Is Democracy Possible*, 146.

13 *Reference re Secession of Quebec*, [1998] 2 S.C.R. 217, para. 153.

14 *Reference re Secession*, para. 149.

15 *Reference re Secession*, para. 64.

16 *Reference re Secession*, para. 68.

17 *Reference re Secession*, para. 64.

18 *Reference re Secession*, paras. 67–77.

19 *Reference re Secession*, paras. 62, 78.

20 See, generally, Wallach, "American Constitutionalism and Democratic Virtue," 219. Nevertheless, as I will argue, the continuation of a governmental context in which elites still hold actual power is very real. See chapter 7 of this volume.

21 The classic framing of this challenge stems from Bickel, *The Least Dangerous Branch*, 16.

22 For the best survey of the different approaches, see Baker, "Constitutional Theory in a Nutshell." There are still judges who offer such platitudinous explanations, including the present Chief Justice of the American Supreme Court. He analogizes what it means to be a judge to being a baseball umpire. See Roberts, "Roberts: 'My Job Is to Call Balls and Strikes and Not to Pitch or Bat.'"

23 Wechsler, "Toward Neutral Principles of Constitutional Law," 19.

24 See, for example, Dworkin, *Law's Empire*.

25 See, for example, Scalia, *A Matter of Interpretation*.

26 See, for example, Sunstein, *Constitutional Personae*; Fallon, *Law and Legitimacy*.

27 See, for example, Ely, *Democracy and Distrust*; Monahan, *Politics and the Constitution*.

28 *Reference re Secession*.

29 See, for example, Tushnet, *Taking the Constitution Away from the Courts*.

3 Constitutional Origins: Undemocratic Beginnings?

1 See Ellis, *American Dialogue*, 159.

2 Parkinson, "What Franklin thought of the Constitution."

3 At this time, the issue of how the Constitution should be interpreted and applied had not yet been seriously addressed and certainly not resolved. See chapter 4 in this volume.

4 Thorpe, *The Constitutional History of the United States*.
5 See the Constitution of the United States, Article V, https://www.senate
   .gov/civics/constitution_item/constitution.html.
6 See the British North America Act, 1867 – Enactment no. 1, https://www
   .justice.gc.ca/eng/rp-pr/csj-sjc/constitution/lawreg-loireg/p1t11.html.
7 Ryerson, *Unequal Union*, 354. For an insightful analysis of Canadian
   constitutionalism's beginnings, see Savoie, *Democracy in Canada*, 42–71.
8 Chrétien, "Towards a New Canadian Constitution." See also Milne, *The
   Canadian Constitution*, and Russell, *Constitutional Odyssey*. For my own
   efforts, see Hutchinson, *Waiting for Coraf*.
9 The British North America Act was largely re-enacted in its entirety and
   renamed the Constitution Act 1867.
10 By legal and political means, Quebec sought to evade the effects of the
    new constitutional compact. However, the Supreme Court ultimately
    ruled that Quebec was bound by the Constitution. Consequently, Quebec
    was legally bound by the Constitution Act. Also, there were several
    attempts by the federal government to remedy the situation, including
    the Meech Lake and Charlottetown Accords, but none succeeded. Also,
    Quebec's efforts to bring about constitutional separation have also been
    scuttled.
11 See chapter 4 in this volume.
12 For a more wide-ranging account of the override provision and its role,
    see chapter 5 in this volume.
13 *Reference re Secession of Quebec*, [1998] 2 S.C.R. 217, para. 72.
14 See, for example, Tribe, *The Invisible Constitution*; Amar, *America's
    Unwritten Constitution*.
15 *Marbury v. Madison*, 5 U.S. 137.
16 See, for example, *British Columbia (Attorney General) v. Christie*, 2007 SCC
    21, [2007] 1 S.C.R. 873. For fuller discussion of the Quebec Reference case,
    see chapter 2 in this volume.
17 For a more extensive critique of constitutional adjudication generally, see
    chapter 5 in this volume.
18 Cairns, "The Politics of Constitutional Conservatism," 38.

4 A Higher Justice: Some Fundamental Problems

1 Friedrich, *Transcendent Justice*, 56.
2 Fukuyama, *The End of History*, 118, 211.
3 See, for example, Waluchow, *A Common Law Theory of Judicial Review*; and
   Dworkin, *Justice in Robes*.

4 *Obergefell v. Hodges*, 135 S. Ct. 2584 (2015), at 2598–9 per Kennedy J. This is merely the tip of the iceberg of such references. Other celebrated instances include *Griswold v. Connecticut*, 85 S. Ct. 1678 (1965), at 1682–3 per Goldberg J.; *Planned Parenthood of Se. Pennsylvania v. Casey*, 505 U.S. 833 (1992), 846–7; and *Washington v. Glucksberg*, 521 U.S. 702 (1997). The source can be found in *Butchers' Union Slaughter-House & Live-Stock Landing Co. v. Crescent City Live-Stock Landing & Slaughter-House Co.*, 111 U.S. 746 (1884), 764–5.

5 See *Saumur v. Quebec (City)*, [1953] 2 S.C.R. 299; and *Roncarelli v. Duplessis*, [1959] S.C.R. 121. For a more recent rendition of this theme, see *Lalonde v. Ontario (Commission de restructuration des services de santé)* (2001), 56 O.R. (3d) 577 (CA) per Weiler and Sharpe JJ.

6 *Sauvé v. Canada (Chief Electoral Officer)*, 2002 SCC 68, [2002] 3 S.C.R. 519, para. 13; see also *Singh v. Canada (Minister of Employment and Immigration)*, [1985] 1 S.C.R. 177; *Manitoba Language Rights Reference*, [1992] 1 SCR 212; and *Ontario (AG) v. Fraser*, 2011 SCC 20, [2011] 2 S.C.R. 3. The most expansive account is in *Reference Re Secession of Quebec*, [1998] 2 SCR 217.

7 See, for example, Monahan, *Politics and the Constitution*.

8 Laskin, "An Inquiry into the Diefenbaker Bill of Rights."

9 Ely, *Democracy and Distrust*, 59.

10 See *Christie v. The York Corporation*, [1940] S.C.R. 139, 142 and 150. I recognize that the licencing body might itself be subject to the Charter and so enforce those requirements in its decision to license any premises. Nevertheless, my basic claim holds – private rights can trump public values. Even the dissenting view of Justice Davis has still not gained traction in Canada today because the courts have not been prepared to stretch the constitution to cover private activities licences by government.

11 See, for example, Cohen, *Supreme Inequality*.

12 See *RJR-Macdonald Inc. v. Canada (Attorney General*, [1995] 3 S.C.R. 199; and *Burwell v. Hobby Lobby*, 573 U.S. 682 (2014).

13 *Slaight Communications Inc. v. Davidson*, [1989] 1 S.C.R. 1038, at 1056.

14 *Goldberg v. Kelly*, 397 U.S. 254 (1970).

15 *Dandridge v. Williams*, 397 U.S. 471 (1970). For the most compelling account of welfare rights in constitutional thinking, see Michelman, "Foreword: On Protecting the Poor through the Fourteenth Amendment."

16 *Gosselin. v. Quebec*, 2002 SCC 84, [2002] 4 S.C.R. 429, at para. 81.

17 *Chaoulli v. Quebec*, 2005 SCC 35, [2005] 1 S.C.R. 791; and *National Federation of Independent Business v. Sebelius*, 567 U.S. 519 (2012).

5 Making Changes: Constitutional Updates

1 As regards Canada, although its Constitution went largely unamended for over 115 years, the introduction of the Charter of Rights in 1982 did not so much amend the constitution as add to it; the existing parts remained largely unchanged.

2 Elkins, Ginsburg, and Melton, *Endurance of National Constitutions*, 2, 131, 137.

3 Elkins, Ginsburg, and Melton, 207.

4 Elkins, Ginsburg, and Melton, 35.

5 Elkins, Ginsburg, and Melton, 38.

6 The best and most rigorous analysis of the whole amendment process is Albert, *Constitutional Amendments*.

7 See Elkins, Ginsburg, and Melton, *Endurance*, 102; see also Lutz, "Toward a Theory of Constitutional Amendment," 260.

8 See chapter 3 in this volume.

9 Hutchinson and Colon-Rios, "Constitutionalising the Senate."

10 For a more sympathetic defence of s. 33, see chapter 3 of this volume.

11 Gerken, "The Hydraulics of Constitutional Reform," 933.

12 See *Brown v. Board of Education*, 347 U.S. 483 (1954); *Roe v. Wade*, 410 U.S. 113 (1973); *Halpern v. Canada (AG)*, [2003] 225 D.L.R. (4th) 529; and *Carter v. Canada (AG)*, [2015] 1 S.C.R. 331.

13 See Strauss, "The Irrelevance of Constitutional Amendment"; Post and Siegel, "Protecting the Constitution from the People."

14 For a detailed account of the historical reliance on these devices, see Hutchinson, *Evolution and the Common Law*, 235–70.

15 The best survey of the different approaches remains Baker, "Constitutional Theory in a Nutshell"; see also, chapter 8 in this volume.

16 Wechsler, "Toward Neutral Principles of Constitutional Law," 19; see also Sunstein, *Constitutional Personae*.

17 *Southern Pacific Co. v. Jensen*, 244 U.S. 205 (1917), 222, per Holmes J.

18 McLachlin, "Of Power, Democracy, and the Judiciary," 21, 25, 27.

19 Roberts Jr., "Roberts's Opening Statement before Senate Panel."

20 Ely, *Democracy and Distrust*, 67.

21 See, for example, Friedman, *The Will of the People*.

22 See, for example, Dworkin, *A Matter of Principle*.

23 See, for example, Tushnet, *Red, White and Blue*. It should be obvious that this book takes such a view; see Hutchinson, *Toward an Informal Account of Legal Interpretation*.

24 The primary work is Segal and Spaeth, *The Supreme Court and the Attitudinal Model Revisited*; see also Muttart, *The Empirical Gap in*

Jurisprudence, and Alarie and Green, "Interventions at the Supreme Court of Canada."

25 Macfarlane, *Governing from the Bench*, 183; see also Songer, *Law, Ideology and Collegiality*, 152.

26 Gibson, "From Simplicity to Complexity," 9.

27 Wetstein and Ostberg, *Value Change in the Supreme Court of Canada*, 286.

28 See, for example, Hirschl, *Towards Juristocracy*.

6 Striving for Democracy: An Endless Journey?

1 For a more philosophical defence of democracy, see Hutchinson, *The Province of Jurisprudence Democratized*.

2 See, for example, Pettit, *Republicanism*, and Pettit, *On the People's Terms*.

3 Barber, *Strong Democracy*, 145–50.

4 Dawson et al., *The Federalist*, see chap. 3.

5 *House of Commons Debates*, 33–1, No. 3 (10 May 1985) at 4611 (Right Hon. Brian Mulroney (Prime Minister)). For a biting critique along these lines, see Mounk, *The People vs. Democracy*, 54–7, 80–98.

6 For an up-to-date survey of participation rates, see Van Reybrouck, *Against Elections*.

7 de Tocqueville, *Democracy in America*, vol. 2, 662.

8 Lawrence, "Justice, Democracy, Litigation, and Political Participation," 466.

9 Ginsburg and Versteeg, "Why Do Countries Adopt Constitutional Review?" 587.

10 Canada, Parliament, *Minutes of Proceedings and Evidence of the Special Joint Committee of the Senate and of the House of Commons on the Constitution of Canada*, 110.

11 See chapter 4 of this volume; see also, Hutchinson, *Toward an Informal Account*.

12 See Arthurs, "Constitutional Courage."

13 Waldron, "The Core of the Case against Judicial Review," 1406.

14 See chapter 10 of this volume.

7 An Elite Concern: Inequality and Democracy

1 de Tocqueville, *Democracy in America*, vol. 2, 662–5. For a more current, but similar view, see Stiglitz, *The Price of Inequality*.

2 For an early critique of how democracy is used to justify authoritarianism, see Wolin, *Democracy Incorporated*; Rowbottom, *Democracy Distorted*.

3 For a more theoretical development and defence of these claims, see Hutchinson, *The Province of Jurisprudence Democratized*.

4 Levitsky and Ziblatt, *How Democracies Die*, 8; see also Brown, *In the Ruins of Neoliberlism*.

5 Martin, "Democracy in the Politics of Aristotle," 1279b40–1280b5, See also Kapstein and Converse, "Poverty, Inequlity, and Democracy," 57; Gilens and Page, "Testing Theories of American Politics," 565.

6 Osberg, *The Age of Increasing Inequality*.

7 See McDonald, "Voter Turnout Demographics."

8 *Citizens United v. Federal Election Commission*, 558 U.S. 310 (2010).

9 Lenin, *State and Revolution*, 23.

10 For a broad and multi-faceted inquiry, see Rovira Kaltwasser et al., *The Oxford Handbook of Populism*.

11 Roosevelt, "FDR's 1944 Speech: A Second Bill of Rights."

12 Deneen et al., *Why Liberalism Failed*, xxvi. There is a large body of recent literature that strives to explain this populist backlash in terms of liberal democracy's implosion. See Mudde and Rovira Kaltwasser, *Populism: A Very Short Introduction*; Kennedy, "A Left of Liberal Interpretation of Trump's 'Big' Win"; Eatwell and Goodwin, *National Populism*; Taylor, *Democracy May Not Exist*.

13 I have dealt with this throughout the book. Indeed, it forms a large part of its central thesis and argument. See chapters 2, 3, 4, and 5.

14 See chapter 4.

15 *Buckley v. Valeo*, 424 U.S. 1 (1976) at 48–9. See also *First National Bank v. Bellotti*, 435 U.S. 765 (1978).

16 *Citizens United v. Federal Election Commission*, 558 U.S. 310 (2010). See also *McCutcheon v. F.E.C.*, 572 U.S. 185 (2014).

17 "Support for Current Constitution Hits 10-Year Low," *Rasmussen Reports*.

18 Sinha, "Canadian Identity, 2013."

19 Siekierski, "Vast Majority of Canadians Trust Supreme Court."

20 Ely, *Democracy and Distrust*, 67.

8 Towards "Democratic Courts": A Salvage Operation

1 Ely, *Democracy and Distrust*, 74.

2 *U.S. v. Carolene Products*, 304 U.S. 144 (1938) at 155n4.

3 Ely, *Democracy and Distrust*, 59.

4 Monahan, *Politics and the Constitution*, 103.

5 Monahan, 12.

6 Monahan, 102, 105.

7 Monahan, 135.

8 Ely, *Democracy and Distrust*, 67.
9 See chapters 6 and 7 in this volume.
10 I would consider myself as someone who runs the strong critical line (i.e., law is politics) that Fallon seems to caricature as cynical. See Hutchinson, *It's All in the Game*; and Hutchinson, *Toward an Informal Account*.
11 Fallon, *Law and Legitimacy*, 11, 38, 80, 130, 159.
12 Sunstein, *Constitutional Personae*, xci, 17, 44, 70, 107. See also, Strauss, "Foreword."
13 *Brown v. Board of Education*, 347 U.S. 483; *Roe v. Wade*, 410 U.S. 113; and *Fraser v. Canada* (Attorney General), [2020] SCC 28; *Carter v. Canada* (Attorney General), [2015] SCC 5.
14 Fallon, *Law and Legitimacy*, xxi.
15 Petter, *The Politics of the Charter*.
16 Roach, *The Supreme Court on Trial*, 106. See also Hogg and Bushnell, "The Charter Dialogue between Courts and Legislatures."
17 *Bell ExpressVu Limited Partnership v. Rex*, 2002 SCC 42, [2002] 2 S.C.R. 559, at para. 62.
18 *Doucet-Boudreau v. Nova Scotia*, 2003 SCC 62 [2003] 3 S.C.R. 3, at para. 36.
19 It is reported that Supreme Court judges do not give much weight to this dialogic account as justificatory device. See Macfarlane, *Governing from the Bench*, 185.
20 Kramer, *The People Themselves*, 233, 247. See also Kramer, "The Interest of the Man," 698 ("resisting popular views about the meaning of the Constitution is considered a judicial virtue").
21 Kramer, *The People Themselves*, 251.
22 Tushnet, *Taking the Constitution Away from the Courts*, 42.
23 Tushnet, 183, 181, 187.
24 *Brown v. Allen*, 344 US 443 at 540 (1953) ("we are not final because we are infallible, but we are infallible only because we are final").
25 Tushnet, *Taking the Constitution Away from the Courts*, 175.

9 Beyond Courts: Towards Democratic Institutions

1 See Sager, "Justice in Plain Clothes."
2 Kramer, "Theory of Deliberative Democracy," 698.
3 See, for example, Ewing, "A Theory of Democratic Adjudication." For my own suggestions about how to make the judiciary more representative and accountable in its present form, see Hutchinson, "Looking for the Good Judge: Merit and Ideology."

4 Gardbaum, "Decoupling Judicial Review from Judicial Supremacy."
5 Michelman, "Brennan and Democracy."
6 Waldron, *Law and Disagreement.*
7 Kramer, "Theory of Deliberative Democracy," 698.
8 Thompson, *Writing by Candlelight,* 170.
9 See chapter10 in this volume. In developing these ideas, I have benefited from the work of Eric Ghosh, even though I take issue with some of his specific proposals. See Ghosh, "Deliberative Democracy" and "Judicial Reference to Community Values."
10 Turley, "Unpacking the Court."
11 See chapter 10 in this volume.
12 See chapter 5 in this volume.

10 A Time for Change: Democratic Constitutions

1 See chapter 5 in this volume.
2 See, generally, Van Reybrouck, *Against Elections.*
3 See Burke, "Speech to the Electors of Bristol, November 1774."
4 Madison, *Federalist,* xx.
5 Ellis, *American Dialogue.*
6 Jefferson, "To Samuel Kercheval, Monticello, July 12, 1816."
7 Twenty-five years corresponds to what is now considered to be the length of a generation. See Devine, "How Long Is a Generation?"
8 Holmes "Learning and Science," 139.
9 Fuller, *In Defence of Democracy.*
10 Waldron, *Law and Disagreement.*
11 This goes to the nub of the democratic challenge. See chapter 9 in this volume.
12 See chapter 4 in this volume.
13 See chapter 5 in this volume.
14 Kramer, *The People Themselves,* 234.

11 Laughing and Remembering: Putting Democracy First

1 See Ellis, *American Dialogue.*
2 Fukuyama, *The End of History,* xx. For another view on why democracy can only succeed as "liberal democracy," see Mounk, *The People vs. Democracy.*
3 See, for example, Lessig, *They Don't Represent Us.*
4 de Tocqueville, *Democracy in America,* vol. 1, 52.

5 See Lefort, *Democracy and Political Theory*; Mouffe, *For a Left Populism*.
6 For my own efforts to trace the practical implications of this for the judicial selection process if courts continue to play this role, see Hutchinson, *Toward an Informal Account*.
7 See chapter 1 in this volume.

Bibliography

Alarie, Benjamin R.D., and Andrew J. Green. "Interventions at the Supreme Court of Canada: Accuracy, Affiliation, and Acceptance." *Osgoode Hall Law Journal* 48, nos. 3 & 4 (2010): 381–410.

Albert, Richard. *Constitutional Amendments: Making, Breaking, and Changing Constitutions.* New York: Oxford University Press, 2019.

Amar, Akhil Reed. *America's Unwritten Constitution: The Precedents and Principles We Live By.* New York: Basic Books, 2012.

Arthurs, Harry. "Constitutional Courage." *McGill Law Journal* 49, no. 1 (2003): 1–22.

Baker, Thomas E. "Constitutional Theory in a Nutshell." *The William and Mary Bill of Rights Journal* 13, no. 1 (October 1, 2004): 57–123.

Barber, Benjamin R. *Strong Democracy: Participatory Politics for a New Age.* Berkeley: University of California Press, 2004.

Bickel, Alexander M. *The Least Dangerous Branch: The Supreme Court at the Bar of Politics.* Indianapolis: Bobbs-Merrill, 1962.

Brown, Wendy. *In the Ruins of Neoliberalism: The Rise of Antidemocratic Politics in the West.* New York: Columbia University Press, 2019.

Burke, Edmund. "Speech to the Electors of Bristol (November 3, 1774)." In *The Select Works of Edmund Burke: Miscellaneous Writings,* 3–13. Oxford: Clarendon Press, 1874–8. Reprint, Indianapolis: Liberty Fund, 1999. https://oll-resources.s3.us-east-2.amazonaws.com/oll3/store/titles/659/0005-04_Bk.pdf.

Cairns, Alain. "The Politics of Constitutional Conservatism." In *And No One Cheered: Federalism, Democracy, and the Constitution Act,* edited by Keith Banting and Richard Simeon, chap. 2. Toronto: Methuen Publications, 1983.

Canada, Parliament. *Minutes of Proceedings and Evidence of the Special Joint Committee of the Senate and of the House of Commons on the Constitution of Canada,* 32d Parliament, 1st Session, No. 48, 29 January 1981.

Chrétien, Jean. "Towards a New Canadian Constitution: Federal Positions on the Priority Items." Minutes of Cabinet Meeting, Ottawa, ON, 16 June 1980.

Clymer, Adam. ""Warren B. Rudman, Blunt Senator Who Led Budget Struggle, Dies at 82." *New York Times,* 20 November 2012. https://www .nytimes.com/2012/11/21/us/politics/warren-b-rudman-new -hampshire-senator-dies-at-82.html.

Cohen, Adam. *Supreme Inequality: The Supreme Court's Fifty-Year Battle for a More Unjust America.* New York: Penguin Publishing, 2020.

Dawson, Henry, John Jay, John Hamilton, James Madison, and Alexander Hamilton. *The Federalist : A Collection of Essays in Favor of the New Constitution as Agreed Upon by the Federal Convention, September 17, 1787 : Reprinted from the Original Text/with an Historical Introduction and Notes by Henry B. Dawson. Nineteenth-Century Legal Treatises: US.* New York: C. Scribner, 1863.

Deneen, Patrick J., James Davison Hunter, and John M. Owen. *Why Liberalism Failed.* New Haven, CT: Yale University Press, 2018.

de Tocqueville, Alexis. *Democracy in America.* Edited by Henry Commager, Translated by Henry Reeve. Vol. 2. London: Oxford University Press, 1946.

− *Democracy in America.* Translated and edited by Harvey Claflin Mansfield and Delba Winthrop. Chicago: University of Chicago Press, 2000.

Devine, Donn. "How Long Is a Generation?" Ancestry Learning Centre. Accessed 24 December 2020. https://www.ancestry.ca/learn /learningcenters/default.aspx?section=lib_Generation.

Dworkin, Ronald. *A Matter of Principle.* Cambridge, MA: Harvard University Press, 1985.

− *Law's Empire.* London: Fontana Press, 1986.

− *Freedom's Law: The Moral Reading of the American Constitution.* Cambridge, MA: Harvard University Press, 1996.

− *Is Democracy Possible Here? Principles for a New Political Debate Princeton.* Princeton, NJ: Princeton University Press, 2006.

− *Justice in Robes.* Cambridge, MA: Belknap Press, 2006.

Eatwell, Roger, and Matthew Goodwin. *National Populism: The Revolt against Liberal Democracy.* London: Pelican, 2018.

Elkins, Zacharay, Tom Ginsburg, and James Melton. *The Endurance of National Constitutions.* Cambridge: Cambridge University Press, 2009.

Ellis, Joseph J. *American Dialogue.* New York: Knopf, 2018.

Ely, John Hart. *Democracy and Distrust: A Theory of Judicial Review.* Cambridge. MA: Harvard University Press, 1980.

Ewing, K.D. "A Theory of Democratic Adjudication: Towards a Representative, Accountable and Independent Judiciary." *Alberta Law Review* 38, no. 3 (November 2000): 708–33.

Fallon Jr., Richard H. *Law and Legitimacy in the Supreme Court*. Cambridge, MA: Harvard University Press, 2018.

Friedman, Barry. *The Will of the People: How Public Opinion Has Influenced the Supreme Court and Shaped the Meaning of the Constitution*. New York: Farrar, Straus and Giroux, 2010.

Friedrich, Carl J. *Transcendent Justice: The Religious Dimension of Constitutionalism*. Durham, NC: Duke University Press, 1964.

– *Constitutional Government and Democracy: Theory and Practice in Europe and America*. 4th ed. Boston: Blaisdell Publishing, 1968.

Fukuyama, Francis. *The End of History and the Last Man*. Harmondsworth, UK: Penguin, 1992.

Fuller, Roslyn. *In Defence of Democracy*. Cambridge: Polity Press, 2019.

Gardbaum, Stephen. "Decoupling Judicial Review from Judicial Supremacy." In *Democratizing Constitutional Law: Perspectives on Legal Theory and the Legitimacy of Constitutionalism*, edited by Thomas da Rosa de Bustamante, and Bernardo Gonçalves Fernandes, 93–118. Geneva, Switzerland: Springer, 2016.

Gerken, Heather K. "The Hydraulics of Constitutional Reform: A Skeptical Response to our Undemocratic Constitution." *Drake Law Review* 55, no. 4 (2007): 925–52.

Ghosh, Eric. "Deliberative Democracy and the Counter-majoritarian Difficulty: Considering Constitutional Juries." *Oxford Journal of Legal Studies* 30, no. 2 (July 1, 2010): 327–59.

– "Judicial Reference to Community Values – A Pointer Towards Constitutional Juries?" In *Democratizing Constitutional Law: Perspectives on Legal Theory and the Legitimacy of Constitutionalism*, edited by Thomas da Rosa de Bustamante, and Bernardo Gonçalves Fernandes, 247–71. Geneva, Switzerland: Springer, 2016.

Gibson, James L. "From Simplicity to Complexity: The Development of Theory in the Study of Judicial Behavior." *Political Behavior* 5, no. 1 (1983): 7–49.

Gilens, Martin, and Benjamin I. Page. "Testing Theories of American Politics: Elites, Interest Groups, and Average Citizens." *Perspectives on Politics* 12, no. 3 (September 2014): 564–81.

Gilmore, Grant. *The Ages of American Law*. New Haven: Yale University Press, 1977.

Ginsburg, Tom, and Mila Versteeg. "Why Do Countries Adopt Constitutional Review?" *The Journal of Law, Economics, and Organization* 30, no. 3 (August 2014): 587–622.

Hirschl, Ran. *Towards Juristocracy: The Origins and Consequences of the New Constitutionalism*. Cambridge, MA: Harvard University Press, 2007.

Hogg, Peter, and Alison Bushnell, "The Charter Dialogue between Courts and Legislatures (Or Perhaps the Charter of Rights Isn't Such a Bad Thing After All)." *Osgoode Hall Law Journal* 35, no. 1 (Spring 1997): 75–124.

Holmes, Oliver Wendell. "Learning and Science." In *Collected Legal Papers*, 135–40. New York: Harcourt, Brace and Howe, 1920.

Hutchinson, Allan C. *Waiting for Coraf : A Critique of Law and Rights*. Toronto: University of Toronto Press, 1995.

– *It's All in the Game: A Non-Foundationalist Account of Law and Adjudication*. Durham, NC: Duke University Press, 2000.

– *Evolution and the Common Law*. Cambridge: Cambridge University Press, 2005.

– *The Province of Jurisprudence Democratized*. New York: Oxford University Press, 2008.

– "Looking for the Good Judge: Merit and Ideology." In *The Democratic Dilemma: Reforming Canada's Supreme Court*, edited by Nadia Verrelli, 99–111. Kingston, ON: Intergovernmental Relations, School of Policy Studies, Queen's University, 2013.

– *Toward an Informal Account of Legal Interpretation*. New York: Cambridge University Press, 2016.

Hutchinson, Allan, and Joel Colón-Ríos. "Constitutionalising the Senate: A Modest Democratic Proposal." *McGill Law Journal* 60, no. 4 (2015): 599–603.

Jefferson, Thomas. "To Samuel Kercheval, Monticello, July 12, 1816." The Letters of Thomas Jefferson, 17431826. American History: From Revolution to Reconstruction. Accessed 24 December 2020. http://www.let.rug.nl /usa/presidents/thomas-jefferson/letters-of-thomas-jefferson/jefl246.php.

Kapstein, Ethan B., and Nathan Converse. "Poverty, Inequality, and Democracy: Why Democracies Fail." *Journal of Democracy* 19, no. 4 (2008): 57–68.

Kennedy, Duncan. "A Left of Liberal Interpretation of Trump's 'Big' Win, Part One: Neoliberalism." *Nevada Law Journal Forum* 1, no. 1 (Spring 2017): 98–107.

Kramer, Larry D. *The People Themselves: Popular Constitutionalism and Judicial Review*. Oxford: Oxford University Press, 2004.

– "The Interest of the Man: James Madison, Popular Constitutionalism, and the Theory of Deliberative Democracy." *Valparaiso University Law Review* 41, no. 2 (Winter 2006): 697–754.

Kundera, Milan. *The Book of Laughter and Forgetting*. Translated by Aaron Asher. London: Faber and Faber, 1996.

Laskin, Bora. "An Inquiry into the Diefenbaker Bill of Rights." *Canadian Bar Review* 37, no. 1 (March 1959): 77–134.

Lawrence, Susan E. "Justice, Democracy, Litigation, and Political Participation." *Social Science Quarterly* 72, no. 3 (1991): 464–77.

Lefort, Claude. *Democracy and Political Theory*. Translated by David Macey. Cambridge: Polity in association with Basil Blackwell, 1988.

Lenin, Vladimir Ilyich. *State and Revolution: Marxist Teaching about the Theory of the State and the Tasks of the Proletariat in the Revolution*. New York: International Publishers, 1932.

Lessig, Laurence. *They Don't Represent Us: Reclaiming Democracy*. New York: Dey Street Books, 2019.

Levitsky, Steven, and Daniel Ziblatt. *How Democracies Die*. New York: Crown, 2018.

Lutz, Donald. "Toward a Theory of Constitutional Amendment." In *Responding to Imperfection: The Theory and Practice of Constitutional Amendment*, edited by Sanford Levinson, 237–74. Princeton, NJ: Princeton University Press, 1995.

Macfarlane, Emmett. *Governing from the Bench: The Supreme Court of Canada and the Judicial Role*. Vancouver: UBC Press, 2013.

Maddex, Robert L. *Constitutions of the World*. 2nd ed. Washington, DC: Congressional Quarterly, 2001.

Martin, Thomas R., with Neel Smith and Jennifer F. Stuart, "Democracy in the Politics of Aristotle." In *Dēmos: Classical Athenian Democracy*, edited by C.W. Blackwell. The Stoa: A Consortium for Electronic Publication in the Humanities, 26 July 2003. http://www.stoa.org/demos/article_aristotle_democracy@page=all&greekEncoding=UnicodeC.html.

McDonald, Michael. "Voter Turnout Demographics." United States Election Project, 2020. www.electproject.org/home/voter-turnout/demographics

McIlwain, Charles Howard. *Constitutionalism: Ancient and Modern*. Ithaca, NY: Cornell University Press, 1940.

McLachlin, Beverly. "Of Power, Democracy, and the Judiciary." *Law Society Gazette*, (1991): 20–7.

Michelman, Frank I. "Foreword: On Protecting the Poor through the Fourteenth Amendment." *Harvard Law Review* 83, no. 1 (November 1969): 7–59.

– "Brennan and Democracy: The 1996–97 Brennan Center Symposium Lecture." *California Law Review* 86, no. 3 (1998): 399–427.

Milne, David. *The Canadian Constitution: The Players and the Issues in the Process That Has Led from Patriation to Meech Lake to an Uncertain Future*. 3rd ed. Toronto: J. Lorimer, 1991.

Monahan, Patrick. *Politics and the Constitution: The Charter, Federalism, and the Supreme Court of Canada*. Agincourt, ON: Carswell, 1987.

Mouffe, Chantal. *For a Left Populism*. London: Verso, 2018.

Mounk, Yasch. *The People vs. Democracy: Why Our Freedom Is in Danger and How to Save It*. Cambridge, MA: Harvard University Press, 2018.

Mudde, Cas, and Cristóbal Rovira Kaltwasser. *Populism: A Very Short Introduction* New York: Oxford University Press, 2017.

Muttart, Daved M. *The Empirical Gap in Jurisprudence: A Comprehensive Study of the Supreme Court of Canada*. Toronto: University of Toronto Press, 2007.

Osberg, Lars. *The Age of Increasing Inequality: The Astonishing Rise of Canada's 1%*. Toronto: James Lorimer & Company Ltd., 2018.

Parkinson, Hilary. "What Franklin thought of the Constitution." *Pieces of History* (blog). U.S. National Archives, 17 September 2010. https://prologue.blogs .archives.gov/2010/09/17/what-franklin-thought-of-the-constitution/.

Petter, Andrew. *The Politics of the Charter: The Illusive Promise of Constitutional Rights*. Toronto: University of Toronto Press, 2010.

Pettit, Philip. *Republicanism: A Theory of Freedom and Government*. Oxford: Oxford University Press, 1997.

– *On the People's Terms: A Republican Theory and Model of Democracy*. Cambridge: Cambridge University Press, 2012.

Post, Robert C., and Reva B. Siegel, "Protecting the Constitution from the People: Juricentric Restrictions on Section Five Power." *Indiana Law Journal* 78, no. 1 (Winter/Spring 2003): 1–46.

Pound, Roscoe. "Law in Books and Law in Action." *American Law Review* 44, no. 1 (January–February 1910): 12–36.

Rawls, John. "The Idea of Public Reason Revisited." *University of Chicago Law Review* 64, no. 3 (Summer 1997): 765–807.

Repplier, Agnes. *Counter-Currents*. Boston: H. Mifflin, 1919.

Roach, Kent. *The Supreme Court on Trial: Judicial Activism or Democratic Dialogue*. Toronto: Irwin Law, 2001.

Roberts, John. "Roberts: 'My Job Is to Call Balls and Strikes and Not to Pitch or Bat." *CNN*, 12 September 2005. www.cnn.com/2005/POLITICS/09/12/roberts.statement/.

Roberts Jr., John G. "Roberts's Opening Statement before Senate Panel." *New York Times*, 12 September 2005. www.nytimes.com/2005/09/12/politics/politicsspecial/robertss-opening-statement-before-senate-panel.html.

Roosevelt, Franklin D. "FDR's 1944 Speech: 'A Second Bill of Rights.'" The Franklin Delano Roosevelt Foundation. 2 August 2016. https://fdrfoundation.org/a-second-bill-of-rights-video/.

Rovira Kaltwasser, Cristóbal, Paul A. Taggart, Paulina Ochoa Espejo, and Pierre Ostiguy. *The Oxford Handbook of Populism*. Oxford: Oxford University Press, 2017.

Rowbottom, Jacob. *Democracy Distorted: Wealth, Influence and Democratic Politics*. Cambridge: Cambridge University Press, 2010.

Russell, Peter H. *Constitutional Odyssey: Can Canadians Become a Sovereign People?* 2nd ed. Toronto: University of Toronto Press, 1993.

Ryerson, Stanley Bréhaut. *Unequal Union: Confederation and the Roots of Conflict in the Canadas, 1815–1873*. Toronto: Progress Books, 1968.

Sager, Lawrence G. "Justice in Plain Clothes: Reflections on the Thinness of Constitutional Law." *Northwestern University Law Review* 88, no. 1 (1993–4): 410–35.

Savoie, Donald J. *Democracy in Canada: The Disintegration of Our Institutions*. Montreal: McGill-Queen's University Press, 2019.

Scalia, Antonin. *A Matter of Interpretation : Federal Courts and the Law*. Edited by Amy Gutmann. Princeton, NJ: Princeton University Press, 1998.

Scruton, Roger. *A Dictionary of Political Thought*. New York: Harper, 1982.

Segal, Jeffrey Allan., and Harold J. Spaeth. *The Supreme Court and the Attitudinal Model Revisited*. Cambridge: Cambridge University Press, 2002.

Siekierski, BJ. "Vast Majority of Canadians Trust Supreme Court, Including Most Tories." iPolitics, 6 August 2015. https://ipolitics.ca/2015/08/16/vast-majority-of-canadians-trust-supreme-court-including-most-tories/.

Sinha, Maire. "Canadian Identity, 2013." Statistics Canada, 1 October 2015. https://www150.statcan.gc.ca/n1/pub/89-652-x/89-652-x2015005-eng.html.

Songer, Donald R. *Law, Ideology, and Collegiality: Judicial Behaviour in the Supreme Court of Canada*. Montreal: McGill-Queen's University Press, 2012.

Stiglitz, Joseph E. *The Price of Inequality: How Today's Divided Society Endangers Our Future*. New York: W.W. Norton, 2012.

Strauss, David A. "The Irrelevance of Constitutional Amendments." *Harvard Law Review* 114, no. 5 (March 2001): 1457–505.

– Foreword to "Does the Constitution Mean What It Says." *Harvard Law Review* 129, no. 1 (November 2015): 1–61.

Sunstein, Cass. *Constitutional Personae: Heroes, Soldiers, Minimalists, and Mutes*. New York: Oxford University Press, 2015.

"Support for Current Constitution Hits 10-Year Low." *Rasmussen Reports*, 11 October 2017. www.rasmussenreports.com/public_content/politics/general_politics/october_2017/support_for_current_constitution_hits_10_year_low.

Taylor, Astra. *Democracy May Not Exist, But We'll Miss It When It's Gone*. New York: Metropolitan Books, 2019.

Thompson, E.P. *Writing by Candlelight*. London: Merlin Press, 1980.

Thorpe, Francis Newton. *The Constitutional History of the United States 1765–1895*. New York: Da Capo Press, 1970.

Tribe, Laurence H. *The Invisible Constitution*. New York: Oxford University Press, 2008.

Turley, Jonathan. "Unpacking the Court: The Case for the Expansion of the United States Supreme Court in the Twenty-First Century." *Perspectives on Political Science* 33, no. 3 (July 1, 2004): 155–62.

Tushnet, Mark V. *Red, White, and Blue : A Critical Analysis of Constitutional Law*. Cambridge, MA: Harvard University Press, 1988.

– *Taking the Constitution Away from the Courts*. Princeton, NJ: Princeton University Press, 1999.

Van Reybrouck, David. *Against Elections: The Case for Democracy*. London: Bodley Head, 2017.

Waldron, Jeremy. *Law and Disagreement*. Oxford: Clarendon Press, 1999.

– "The Core of the Case against Judicial Review." *Yale Law Journal* 115, no. 6 (April 2006): 1346–407.

Wallach, John R. "American Constitutionalism and Democratic Virtue." *Ratio Juris* 15, no. 3 (September 2002): 219–41.

Waluchow, Wilfrid J. *A Common Law Theory of Judicial Review: The Living Tree*. Cambridge: Cambridge University Press, 2007.

Wechsler, Herbert. "Toward Neutral Principles of Constitutional Law." *Harvard Law Review* 73, no. 1 (November 1959): 1–35.

Wetstein, Matthew E., and C.L. Ostberg. *Value Change in the Supreme Court of Canada*. Toronto: University of Toronto Press, 2017.

Wolin, Sheldon S. *Democracy Incorporated: Managed Democracy and the Specter of Inverted Totalitarianism*. Princeton, NJ: Princeton University Press, 2008.

Index

UTP insights

- Allan C. Hutchinson, *Democracy and Constitutions: Putting Citizens First*
- Paul Nelson, *Global Development and Human Rights: The Sustainable Development Goals and Beyond*
- Harvey P. Weingarten, *Nothing Less than Great: Reforming Canada's Universities*
- Peter H. Russell, *Sovereignty: The Biography of a Claim*
- Alistair Edgar, Rupinder Mangat, and Bessma Momani, *Strengthening the Canadian Armed Forces through Diversity and Inclusion*
- David B. MacDonald, *The Sleeping Giant Awakens: Genocide, Indian Residential Schools, and the Challenge of Conciliation*
- Paul W. Gooch, *Course Correction: A Map for the Distracted University*
- Paul T. Phillips, *Truth, Morality, and Meaning in History*
- Peter MacKinnon, *University Commons Divided: Exploring Debate and Dissent on Campus*
- Raisa B. Deber, *Treating Health Care: How the System Works and How It Could Work Better*
- Jim Freedman, *A Conviction in Question: The First Trial at the International Criminal Court*
- Christina D. Rosan and Hamil Pearsall, *Growing a Sustainable City? The Question of Urban Agriculture*
- John Joe Schlichtman, Jason Patch, and Marc Lamont Hill, *Gentrifier*
- Robert Chernomas and Ian Hudson, *Economics in the Twenty-First Century: A Critical Perspective*
- Stephen M. Saideman, *Adapting in the Dust: Lessons Learned from Canada's War in Afghanistan*
- Michael R. Marrus, *Lessons of the Holocaust*
- Roland Paris and Taylor Owen (eds.), *The World Won't Wait: Why Canada Needs to Rethink its International Policies*
- Bessma Momani, *Arab Dawn: Arab Youth and the Demographic Dividend They Will Bring*
- William Watson, *The Inequality Trap: Fighting Capitalism Instead of Poverty*
- Phil Ryan, *After the New Atheist Debate*
- Paul Evans, *Engaging China: Myth, Aspiration, and Strategy in Canadian Policy from Trudeau to Harper*

www.ingramcontent.com/pod-product-compliance
Lightning Source LLC
Chambersburg PA
CBHW020253030426
42336CB00010B/740